Journeys in Time

A New Atlas of American History

Elspeth Leacock and Susan Buckley

Illustrations by Rodica Prato

HOUGHTON MIFFLIN COMPANY
BOSTON 2001

www.houghtonmifflinbooks.com

The text of this book is set in Times Roman.
Book design by Kevin Ullrich

Library of Congress Cataloging-in-Publication Data

Leacock, Elspeth.
Journeys in time : a new atlas of American history / written by Elspeth
Leacock and Susan Buckley ; illustrated by Rodica Prato.
p.   cm.
ISBN 0-395-97956-0
1. United States — History — Miscellanea — Juvenile literature.
2. United States — Historical geography — Juvenile literature. 3. United
States — Historical geography — Maps for children. 4. Children's
atlases. [1. United States — History. 2. Atlases.] I. Buckley, Susan. II.
Prato, Rodica, ill. III. Title.
E179.5 .B95 2001
973 — dc21
00-040803

Printed in Singapore
TWP 10 9 8 7 6 5 4 3 2 1

*To Rich, Cheyenne, and Willy—who taught me
a way of seeing that brought me to this book*

—E. L.

For Peter and the journey we took

—S. B.

Note to the Reader

You will notice both double and single quotation marks in this book.
We use double quotation marks when we know exactly what someone
said. We use single quotation marks when we have invented statements
based on historical evidence.

Introduction

Journeys in Time is an atlas, a book of maps. Maps tell the stories of history in their own way. On a map you can trace a route, understand the shape of the land, and see a story in the spaces where it unfolded.

America's history is the story of people on the move. The first Americans peopled the continent "back in the beforetime" and over thousands of years. Others came and traveled as explorers and as settlers, free and enslaved. Their descendents moved out across America. Some sought adventure. Others went toward freedom. And always, new Americans have followed in the footsteps of those who journeyed before them.

History is the story of all of the lives lived today and in the past. Your story and your family's story are part of the history of this nation. Some of our stories are grand adventures, and some are small tragedies. Some change the lives of nations. Others touch one child alone.

Each of the journeys in this book is a true story. We invite you to add your journeys to this American history that we all share.

Contents

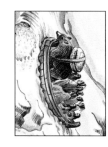

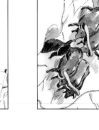

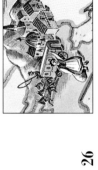

How the Anishinabe Found a New Home

Lake Michigan

Lake Superior

Lake Huron

Lake Erie

Lake Ontario

Great (Niagara) Falls

THE ANISHINABE

Long Ago

Up, up through the Hole-in-the-Sky, Nanabush went in search of the Great Spirit. Floods covered the land below, and the People were in trouble. 'The Anishinabe—the People—have not followed the way of goodness,' the Great Spirit said sadly. Nanabush, Teacher of the People, pleaded with the Great Spirit. 'Give the Anishinabe another chance,' he begged. Finally, the Great Spirit agreed to give them the Gift of Life once more. 'Lead the Anishinabe toward the setting sun,' he directed. 'Find a turtle-shaped island where food grows on water. There the Anishinabe will make a new home.'

hear the roar of a great waterfall ahead. Now Nanabush asked Shibje to help them get through the rapids and past the Great Falls. **5** First Shibje sprinkled herbs on the water to watch the direction and speed in which they floated away. Then he put his ear close down to the river, and he listened. 'The louder the sound, the closer the falls,' Shibje said.

Bear, Nanabush, and the Anishinabe traveled along the Blue Way past the falls, over one lake and then another. At the end of the third lake, they found another turtle-shaped island. **6** Once again they settled and began to look for food that grows on water. They found little food of any kind on this island, though. When the cold winds of winter began to blow, Windigo, the Eater of Man, appeared. With his icy fur and icicle teeth, Windigo drove the People away.

Crossing to the shore, the Anishinabe tried to settle where there were fish to catch and eat. **7** Here Bear left them, for it was the time of his long sleep. He gave the Sacred Shell to Otter, who could swim with it on his back. Now Otter led the way as Nanabush and the People traveled on the greatest lake of them all. **8** Waves tossed the canoes as if they were back on the Great Salt Water.

Finally, the Anishinabe reached a small turtle-shaped island at the end of the lake. **9** As they approached, sandhill cranes filled the sky. The shrieking birds swooped down over the grasses that waved in the lake, beating them against the birchbark canoes. A shower of grain poured into the boats. Here, at last, was the food that grows on water. Here was *minomin*, wild rice, the good seed. The Anishinabe had found their new home.

ANISHINABE FACTS

- *Anishinabe means "original man." The Anishinabe are a group of Native American people who all speak the same language.*
- *The Anishinabe people migrated from the eastern coast of North America to the Great Lakes area, perhaps as long as 12,000 years ago.*
- *Wild rice, the "food that grows on water," is still harvested by Anishinabe people today.*

When Nanabush returned to the earth, he brought the Gift of Life in a Sacred Shell. Knowing that the journey west would be a hard one, Nanabush asked powerful Bear to carry the shell and to lead the way. And so the Anishinabe set out from the Great Salt Water. **1** They left behind a small group—the Daybreak People—to greet the rising sun each morning.

Shaking his great head from side to side, Bear broke through the thick forest of trees to lead Nanabush and the Anishinabe across the mountains. **2** When they reached the wide river, they found a turtle island **3** and decided to stay. The Anishinabe built wigwams, birchbark lodges to live in. But they found no food growing on water. So they moved on.

Always carrying the Sacred Shell, Bear led Nanabush and the Anishinabe along the Blue Way **4** toward the setting sun. The People traveled in birchbark canoes, one of the Anishinabe's gifts to the world. As they paddled up the river, they could

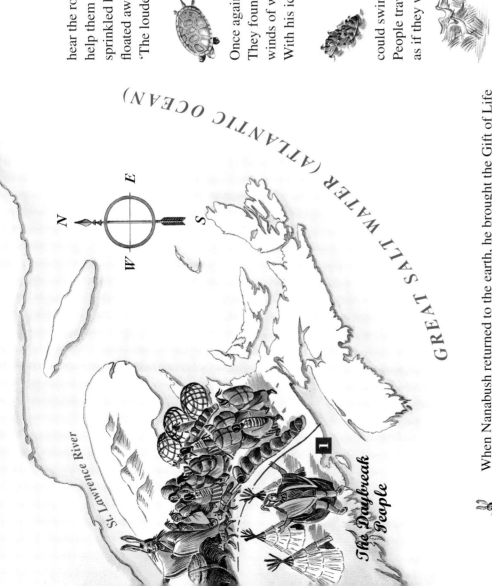

GREAT SALT WATER (ATLANTIC OCEAN)

St. Lawrence River

The Daybreak People

1

Ship's Boy with Christopher Columbus

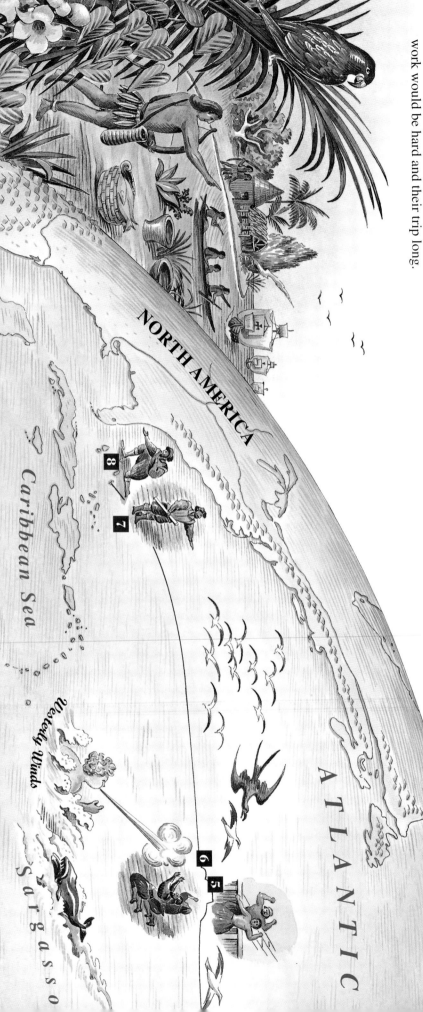

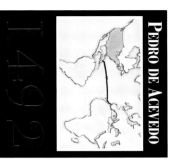

1492

Blessed be the light of day, and He who sends the night away," Pedro de Acevedo sang out to the sailors on the *Santa María*. As the sun rose over the ocean, it was the job of the ship's boys like Pedro to lead the morning prayers. "God give us good days, good voyage, good passage to the ship," he prayed. It was August 1492, and Pedro de Acevedo was sailing with Christopher Columbus.

Three ships—the *Santa María*, the *Niña*, the *Pinta*—set sail from Palos, Spain, before sunrise on August 3. **1** They were sailing west across the Atlantic on the great adventure organized by Columbus. He called it the Enterprise of the Indies, for reaching Asia was his goal. Of the 90 men and boys on board, 16 were ship's boys like Pedro. On that soft summer morning, they knew that their work would be hard and their trip long.

Just three days out, the rudder that steered the *Pinta* slipped out of position. The Enterprise of the Indies had to wait for the repair in the Canary Islands. Not until September 6 could the three ships start their journey west. By September 9 they were out of sight of land. Some sailors sighed, others cried, terrified that they would never see their homes again. **2**

Christopher Columbus was a fine sailor. He had his ships steered to catch the winds that blew west across the sea. The waters were gentle, but the sailors were frightened. Never before had anyone in their world sailed so far from land. They hoped that each flock of birds **3** was a sign that land was near. They feared that a shooting star **4** was a sign of disaster.

Pedro de Acevedo was too young and too busy to worry like the older sailors. Every half-hour the ship's boys turned the sand-filled glasses that kept the time. With each turn there were special songs to sing, to announce the hour. Ship's boys helped care for the all-important compasses and filled in leaking holes to keep the ships afloat. They scrubbed the decks and trimmed the lamps. And once a day, at 11 A.M., they served the hot meal they had cooked.

On and on the ships sailed. Pushed by the winds, they made their way through the thick midocean weeds called the Sargasso Sea. When the winds died down on September 20, Columbus changed course until the ships were blown west again. Still they sailed on. By September 25 worried sailors wanted to throw Columbus overboard and turn toward home. **5** Then at sunset the *Pinta's* captain cried out that he saw land. **6** By sunrise, however, the sailors realized that the longed-for land was only clouds.

By October 10 the sailors had had enough. 'We can stand it no longer,' they said, threatening mutiny. Columbus reminded them of their duty to God and their rulers, as well as of the riches that awaited them in Asia. He promised to turn the ships back toward Spain if they had not reached solid ground in three days. **7**

The very next day, signs of land appeared. Reeds floated by. Flocks of birds darkened the sky. As day broke on October 12, Pedro de Acevedo and his fellow sailors looked out across a turquoise sea and saw an island. Unknown to them, the Enterprise of the Indies had reached the Americas, not Asia. **8** For the sailors, for the people whom they encountered, and for the world they had left behind, nothing would ever be the same again.

COLUMBUS FACTS

- *The Santa María was about 77 feet long. The Niña and Pinta were each about 70 feet long.*
- *The three ships sailed 3,200 miles from the Canary Islands to the Caribbean islands in a little more than 33 days.*
- *To determine the speed at which a ship was traveling, sailors measured how fast bubbles or seaweed passed in the water.*
- *Ship's boys were paid about $5 a month.*

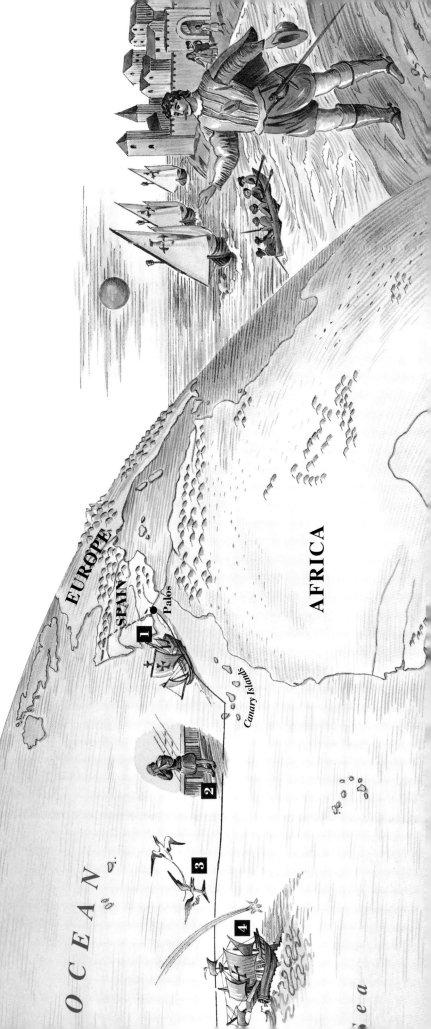

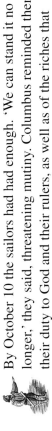

OCEAN

EUROPE

SPAIN

Palos

Canary Islands

AFRICA

Sea

Founding New Mexico

PACIFIC OCEAN

Gulf of California

Colorado River

Arkansas River

Canadian River

Rio Grande

Pecos River

Brazos River

Rio Concho

Mexico City

San Juan

300 miles

N W S E

JUAN DE OÑATE

1598

Armored soldiers on horseback, women and children, cattle, sheep, goats, pigs, oxen, mules, 83 carts, and 2 coaches—the line stretched out for four miles. On January 26, 1598, the expedition of Don Juan de Oñate was bound for the lands the Spanish called New Mexico. A rich Spaniard born in New Spain, Oñate organized and paid for the expedition. With hundreds of colonists and eight priests, he planned to build a settlement, gain wealth and power, and convert the native people to Christianity.

Don Juan de Oñate had waited for this moment for almost three years. He had left the capital at Mexico City **1** in 1595, with permission to form an expedition. In good faith Oñate had assembled the massive number of people, animals, carts, and supplies needed for such an undertaking. And then the governors of New Spain changed their minds. It took several years and all of Oñate's power and skill to regain the right to set out on this journey.

Starting at last in the mountains north of Mexico City, **2** the great caravan moved slowly north in a cloud of dust. It was a journey of extremes. At one moment, soldiers and herders worked side by side to move the vast expedition across a rushing river. Another day, Oñate and his officers celebrated with a banquet, at tables set with silver carried from home.

With no maps to guide the way, Oñate relied on reports from earlier explorers and the aid of the Indians they met. **3** By late April 1598 the caravan had reached the Rio Grande, the southern border of the province of New Mexico. There Don Juan de Oñate took possession of New Mexico, claiming for the Spanish king all things, "from the leaves of the trees in the forests to the stones and sands of the river." **4**

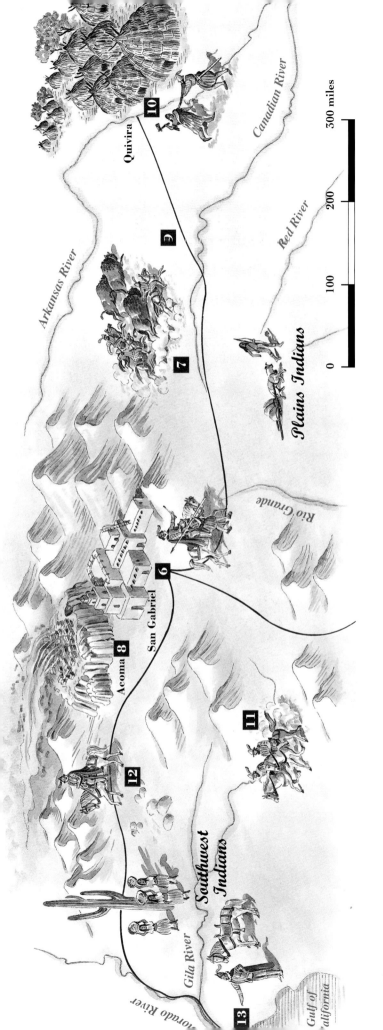

Arkansas River

Quivira

Canadian River

Red River

Rio Grande

Gila River

Colorado River

Gulf of California

San Gabriel

Acoma

Southwest Indians

Plains Indians

0   100   200   300 miles

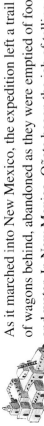

As it marched into New Mexico, the expedition left a trail of wagons behind, abandoned as they were emptied of food and water. In New Mexico, Oñate began the job of telling the native people—who had lived there for hundreds of years—that they and their lands now belonged to Spain. By August he had settled the expedition at a pueblo he called San Juan. **5** With the help of hundreds of Indians, the colonists built a church and began a town, which they named San Gabriel. **6**

And then their misadventures began. Oñate sent soldiers out to capture and fence in the wild buffalo, which he had claimed for the king. **7** But the buffalo would not be contained. Disaster struck when the people of the pueblo at Acoma **8** rebelled against the demands the Spanish made upon them. Oñate's soldiers burned and destroyed the pueblo. More than 600 Acoma people were killed and another 600 taken prisoner.

As the years passed, the colonists—and the leaders in Mexico City—continued to long for riches. In 1601 Oñate decided to travel east to Quivira, rumored to be a city of great wealth. With about 100 Spanish soldiers and more than 700 horses and mules, he marched across the plains. **9** Passing groups of Plains Indians along the way, the caravan finally reached Quivira. **10** There the travelers found the Quivira people, who fought to defend their homes, but they found no gold. When the

Spanish returned to San Gabriel empty-handed five months after they had left, they entered an almost deserted town. Most of the colonists had fled back to Mexico City. **11**

In 1604 Oñate made one last attempt to find riches. With 30 soldiers he traveled west to find the precious pearls he had heard of. **12** Though he reached the Gulf of California, **13** he found no pearls. Oñate never found the riches he had hoped for, but his colony endured. Before Jamestown, before Plymouth, Don Juan de Oñate had founded a colony that would one day become a state.

JUAN DE OÑATE FACTS

- *The Spanish title don stands for the first letters of "de origen noble," which means "of noble origin" in Spanish.*

- *The wife of Juan de Oñate was the granddaughter of the Spanish conquistador Hernán Cortés.*

- *Juan de Oñate's journey north from Rio Concho took seven months and was 800 miles long.*

- *Santa Fe became the capital of the New Mexico colony in 1610. It is the oldest capital in the United States.*

The Voyage of the MAYFLOWER

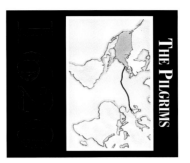

THE PILGRIMS

O ne windy fall day—September 6, 1620— a small and very crowded ship set sail from the port of Plymouth, England. The passengers on board were 102 women, men, and children. They carried with them a few of their possessions and all of their dreams for building new lives in America. The ship was the *Mayflower*, and the brave travelers were the Pilgrims, who would settle the colony of New Plymouth.

Leading the group were 39 Separatists, who wanted to separate from the Church of England in order to worship the way they wished. Others were traveling for different reasons—to find something in the new land or to escape from something in the old. The Separatists called these 40 people Strangers. The rest of the travelers came as servants or hired hands. About one third of the passengers were children. Among them were Resolved White, Desire Minter, Love Brewster, Remember Allerton, Will Latham, and Humility Cooper.

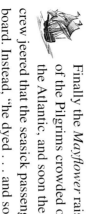

The group had set out first in two ships, the *Speedwell* and the *Mayflower*. It was dangerous for one small ship to cross the Atlantic alone, and neither ship seemed large enough to hold everyone. But the *Speedwell* was not a very good boat. Twice it sprang a leak, and all the travelers had to turn back to England.

Finally the *Mayflower* raised anchor and set out alone. **1** with all of the Pilgrims crowded on board. It was late in the year to cross the Atlantic, and soon the seas were rough. A bully in the ship's crew jeered that the seasick passengers would die and be thrown overboard. Instead, "he dyed . . . and so was him selfe the first that was throwne overboard." **2**

It was hurricane season, and the storms grew fiercer. When a main beam cracked, many thought their journey would end at the bottom of the sea. But the

Pilgrims had with them a large iron screw. They used it to prop up the beam, and the ship was saved. **3**

One life almost ended and another life began. When John Howland was swept overboard, he grabbed a rope and was saved. **4** A few days later, Oceanus Hopkins was born, a new brother for Damaris, Constance, and Giles. **5**

Gale winds from the south blew the *Mayflower* slightly off course. **6** Bound for Virginia, the ship never got there. It was off the New England coast that birds were first sighted. Land was near, but young William Butten never reached it. Butten died and was buried at sea. **7** Finally, the *Mayflower* anchored in Cape Cod Bay. **8** The trip from England to America had taken 66 days—twice as long as Columbus's first voyage.

NORTH
AMERICA

South Wind

8

7

6

MAYFLOWER FACTS

• **THE SHIP** The Mayflower was about 100 feet long and 24 feet wide at its widest point. From the top deck to the bottom of the ship measured 44 feet. The Mayflower was called "a sweet ship," because it did not stink like most ships of the day. It had carried cargoes of wine for 12 years, so it had a good, fruity smell.

• **THE CREW** About 30 men and boys worked on the ship. Captain Christopher Jones was in charge. There were four mates, four quartermasters, one surgeon, one carpenter, one cooper (to make and to repair barrels), and one cook. The rest were boatswains, gunners, and "men before the mast" (who worked the ropes and sails).

• **THE CARGO** The travelers brought clothes—hats, caps, shirts, neck cloths, jerkins, doublets, waistcoats, breeches, leggings, stockings, shoes, boots, belts. They brought 125 extra pairs of shoes and 13 extra pairs of boots.

• They brought bedding, chests, mattresses, and probably a baby's cradle. And there were pots and kettles, wooden trenchers, jugs, cups, spoons, and knives. The Pilgrims brought seeds to plant and hoes to till the soil in their new home.

• Several hundred books crossed the ocean too. Pilgrim families brought Bibles, hymnals, and copies of sermons that they wanted to remember. On the ship, too, was a history of the world and probably an alphabet primer.

• There were cats on all ships, to catch mice and rats. On the Mayflower there were two dogs, too—a mastiff and a spaniel.

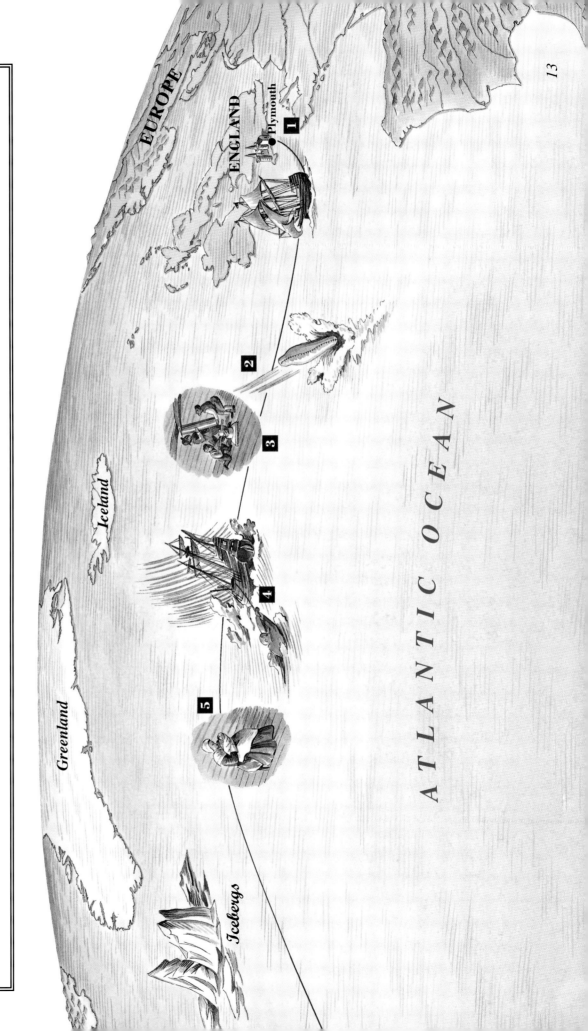

EUROPE

ENGLAND

Plymouth

Iceland

Greenland

Icebergs

ATLANTIC OCEAN

Ben Franklin Goes to Philadelphia

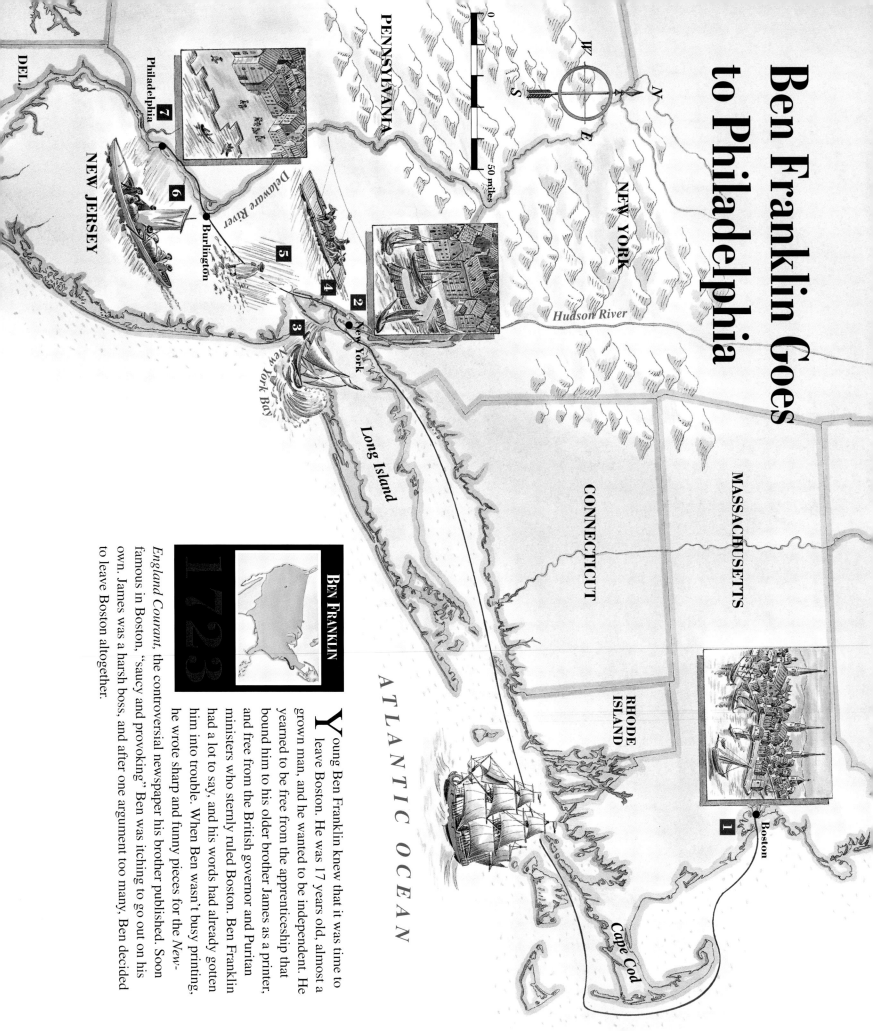

PENNSYLVANIA

NEW YORK

Hudson River

DEL.

NEW JERSEY

Philadelphia **7**

6

Burlington

Delaware River

5

4

3

2 New York

New York Bay

CONNECTICUT

RHODE ISLAND

MASSACHUSETTS

Long Island

ATLANTIC OCEAN

1 Boston

Cape Cod

0   50 miles

BEN FRANKLIN

1723

Young Ben Franklin knew that it was time to leave Boston. He was 17 years old, almost a grown man, and he wanted to be independent. He yearned to be free from the apprenticeship that bound him to his older brother James as a printer, and free from the British governor and Puritan ministers who sternly ruled Boston. Ben Franklin had a lot to say, and his words had already gotten him into trouble. When Ben wasn't busy printing, he wrote sharp and funny pieces for the *New-England Courant*, the controversial newspaper his brother published. Soon famous in Boston, "saucy and provoking" Ben was itching to go out on his own. James was a harsh boss, and after one argument too many, Ben decided to leave Boston altogether.

Ben knew that his father and his brother would try to prevent him from going, for apprentices were bound to serve out their contracts. So he secretly arranged passage on a ship sailing to New York, where he hoped to find work as a printer. On September 25, 1723, Ben Franklin set out from Boston **1** to make his way in the world. With a good wind, the ship reached New York in only three days. New York was just a small town then, at the end of Manhattan Island. **2** Its only printer, William Bradford, told the eager young man that he had no work for him. 'Go to Philadelphia,' he said.

The trip to Philadelphia, only 100 miles, was not simple in 1723. Ben's adventures almost ended when he took a small boat **3** headed for New Jersey. As the boat crossed New York Bay on October 1, a sudden storm ripped its sails and drove it toward Long Island. The unhappy passengers spent the night in the open boat, drenched by ocean spray. Thirty hours after they left New York, they reached New Jersey, tired and wet.

The next morning, his good spirits restored, Ben crossed Raritan Bay by ferry. **4** Then he started out on a 50-mile walk in the rain. **5** By noon he wished he had never left home! Ben walked to the town of Burlington. After buying some gingerbread, he looked for a boat in which to cross the river to Philadelphia. Finally, that evening, he found one. It was a hard trip, though, for the passengers had to row the boat in the windless night. **6** By midnight, they were lost. When daylight finally came, Ben could see Philadelphia across the river. **7**

By nine o'clock he had landed at the Market Street Wharf in Philadelphia. **8** The normally busy streets were quiet on that Sunday morning, October 6. Ben was dirty, tired, and hungry. But most of all, he was curious.

Ben decided to eat first. At a bakery, **9** he bought three puffy rolls, putting one under each arm and eating the third. Young Deborah Read thought Ben a strange sight as he passed. **10** little knowing that she would marry him in a few years. Soon Ben went back to the river to take a drink of water. There he gave his other two rolls to a woman he had crossed the river with. **11** Now the streets were filled with well-dressed people. Curious, Ben followed them into the Quaker Meeting House, where he promptly fell asleep among the silent congregation. **12** When he awoke, he went out to find a place to spend his first night in his new city. **13** Ben Franklin would grow old in Philadelphia. He would become its leading citizen. But now all he wanted was a comfortable bed.

BEN FRANKLIN FACTS

- *Benjamin Franklin was born in Boston in 1706, one of 17 children. He died in Philadelphia in 1790.*
- *A man of incredible talents, Franklin organized the first city hospital in America, the first city mail delivery, and the first subscription library in the world. He invented bifocal glasses, the Franklin stove, and the lightning rod.*
- *Benjamin Franklin played a key role in creating both the Declaration of Independence and the Constitution of the United States.*

Delaware River

Market St.

The Journey of Venture Smith

1739

In an instant, the little boy felt a blow on his head and a rope around his neck. A minute earlier he had been Broteer, the oldest son of the prince of the Dukandarra people of West Africa. Now he was a captive, led off to be sold into slavery. Six-year-old Broteer was captured by the army of a neighboring African people. Terrorizing the countryside, the invaders seized men, women, and children. They killed Broteer's father as he tried to defend his family. Then they dragged Broteer and others away with them. Broteer would never see his home again.

1 The slave capturers marched Broteer away from his homeland, walking 400 miles to the coast. Broteer was a strong boy, but he struggled under the weight of the 25-pound grinding stone he was forced to carry on his head. He was exhausted, and he was very frightened.

2 At Anamaboo on the African coast, Broteer was locked in a castle with hundreds of captives. They all would be sold as slaves to European and American slave traders. The traders came to Africa in ships to buy slaves. This terrible trade in human lives — the Atlantic slave trade — went on for more than 400 years.

After some time, Broteer and other captives were put in a boat and rowed to an American ship waiting in the harbor. **3** There Captain Collingwood and his crew made their choices. Altogether they bought 260 human beings. Most would be resold in American slave markets. Somehow, young Broteer caught the attention of Robertson Mumford, an officer on the ship. Mumford paid four gallons of rum and a piece of calico cloth for the boy. Because it was his own venture, he gave Broteer a new name. From then on, Broteer would be known as Venture.

For the enslaved Africans, the voyage across the Atlantic was ghastly. Belowdecks they were crowded together so closely that they could hardly move.

Slave market in Barbados

NORTH AMERICA

Caribbean Sea

SOUTH AMERICA

Barbados

5

6

7

ATLANTIC

Sanitary conditions were horrible, and often disease swept through a ship. On Venture's passage, 60 people died of smallpox. ▣4 The Africans called this time aboard ship "the middle passage," for it lay between one world and another—between lives of freedom and lives of slavery.

After about six weeks, the ship arrived at the Caribbean island of Barbados. ▣5 In the busy slave markets there, Captain Collingwood sold all but 4 of the 200 Africans still alive on his ship. On islands like Barbados, white owners of sugar plantations bought thousands of Africans to work growing sugarcane and turn it into sugar and rum. Slave traders like Collingwood bought slaves in Africa and sold them in the Caribbean, where they bought rum and took it back to America to sell. Along with his cargo, Captain Collingwood took Venture and three other Africans with him to America. As they sailed north, Venture felt something he had never known before: cold. ▣6

In the British colony of Rhode Island, Venture began his new life. ▣7 It was not a life that he chose, but he made the best of it. He lived in slavery until he was 36 years old, bought and sold four times in all. His last owner, an army colonel, let Venture earn money to buy his freedom. As a free man, Venture took the colonel's name and became known as Venture Smith. In time, he bought the freedom of his wife, Meg, and of their children. He worked hard—farming, digging clams, cutting wood—and by the end of his life he owned 100 acres, three houses, and a fleet of small boats in Connecticut. Before he died, Venture Smith told his story. He told of his incredible journey from freedom to slavery to freedom once again. Of all that had happened, he said, "My freedom is a privilege which nothing else can equal."

SLAVERY FACTS

- *Historians estimate that from 1440 to 1870 more than 11 million African people were sold into slavery in the Atlantic slave trade. About 500,000 Africans were sent to North America.*

- *The first Africans arrived in the American colonies in 1619. They came to Jamestown in Virginia, probably as servants. By the first American census, in 1790, almost 700,000 people of African heritage lived in the United States.*

- *The Constitution of the United States banned the slave trade after the year 1808. An illegal slave trade lasted until 1865, when all slavery was banned in the United States.*

Bhateen's homeland

EUROPE

AFRICA

Anamaboo

OCEAN

Deaths at sea

Daniel Boone Builds the Wilderness Road

DANIEL BOONE

1775

The sound of men chopping wood rang through the lonely Appalachian forest as trees crashed to the ground. Led by frontiersman Daniel Boone, a group of 30 woodsmen were cutting a trail into Kentucky. A few white men had passed this way before, but mostly the land was used for hunting by the Cherokee and Shawnee peoples.

As the colonies grew crowded, folks like Daniel Boone moved west to find better hunting and more space. Some had even grander dreams. Judge Richard Henderson wanted to build a new colony west of the Appalachians. Henderson bought land from the Cherokee. Then he sent Daniel Boone to make the road new settlers would need. **1**

On March 10, 1775, Daniel Boone and the woodsmen set out to build the Wilderness Road. Susannah, Boone's 15-year-old daughter, and Hannah, an African American slave, went along to cook and keep camp. The journey began at the blockhouse near the Holston River. **1**

W N E S

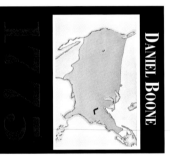

Warrior's Path

Wilderness Road

Kentucky River

Rockcastle River

Dr. Thomas Walker's Cabin

Cumberland Gap

Powell River

Clinch River

Holston River

Martin Station

Block House

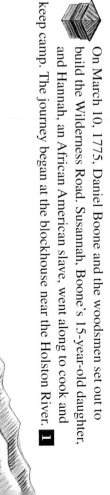

0
30 miles

Boone took the lead, marking the trail and hunting for dinner. **2** He knew where he was going. On earlier trips he had explored the Cumberland Gap. He had traveled the ancient Warrior's Path. He had even picked out a settlement spot on the banks of the Kentucky River.

The road-making group set out in high spirits, though the work was hard and the weather was wet and cold. Past the Cumberland Gap, the men cleared the Warrior's Path for 50 miles. Then they turned off to follow a buffalo trace, or path. They crossed rivers and countless streams. **3** They cut through 20 long miles of hard dead brush **4** and 30 miles of dense cane. **5**

By March 24 the tired travelers were only 15 miles from their destination. Though they were intruding on land long claimed by the Cherokee and Shawnee, none of the woodsmen stood guard as they camped that night. Before dawn, a group of Indians attacked. **6** Felix Walker and William Twitty were badly wounded. Sam, Twitty's African American slave, was killed. In spite of Daniel Boone's careful nursing, William Twitty died.

On April 1 the road makers pressed on for one last day, with Felix Walker on a stretcher. As Daniel Boone led the party toward the river, they saw hundreds of buffalo romping in the meadow below. **7** It was a sight, Walker said, "some of us never saw before nor perhaps may ever again." In just three weeks, Daniel Boone and his woodsmen had opened the Wilderness Road. Now it was time to build a new community on the frontier.

FRONTIER FACTS

- *In 1775 about 400 settlers lived in Kentucky. By 1790 there were 73,000.*
- *Daniel Boone never wore a coonskin cap. He preferred a wide-brimmed felt hat made from beaver fur.*
- *"Kentucky" comes from the Iroquois word ken-ta-kee, meaning "among the meadows."*

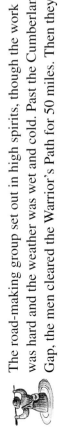

Roanoke River

Jo's Tavern

Smithfield Plantation

Great Wagon Road

New River

Fort House

Settler's Cabin

VIRGINIA

NORTH CAROLINA

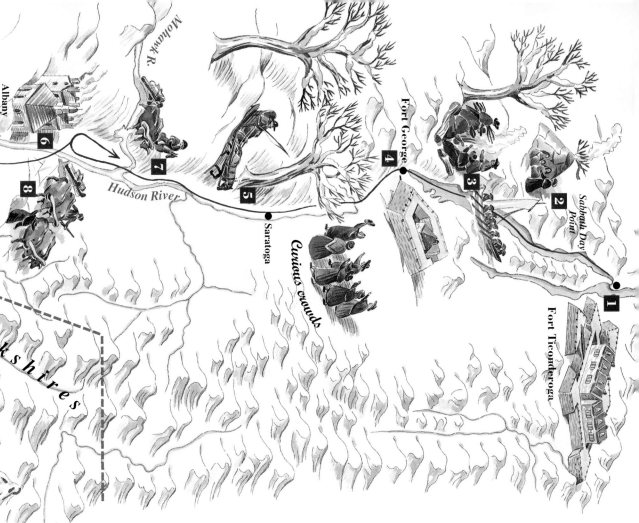

NEW YORK

MASSACHUSETTS

The Berkshires

Hudson River

Mohawk R.

Curious crowds

Albany

Saratoga

Westfield

Springfield

Fort George

Fort Ticonderoga

Sabbath Day Point

Bringing the Big Guns to Boston

Henry Knox had a wild idea. The 25-year-old Boston bookseller was a patriot, and he wanted to support the colonists' cause in the revolution that was just beginning. Bostonians wanted the British out of Boston—and out of America, too. George Washington, new commander of the Continental Army, had only a ragtag collection of soldiers surrounding the town. To win control of Boston he needed big guns, and Henry Knox knew where to get them.

In May 1775, American soldiers had captured Fort Ticonderoga from the British. Sitting there unused was the kind of artillery—cannons, mortars, and howitzers—that General Washington needed. 'We will bring the Ticonderoga guns to Boston,' said Henry Knox.

In mid-November, Knox rode the 300 miles from Boston to Fort Ticonderoga, at the northern end of Lake George. He traveled on horseback with his 19-year-old brother, William. By early December the Knox brothers had reached the fort. **1** There Henry quickly selected 59 pieces of artillery, including 43 cannons, to be taken to Boston. Then the hired crews pushed

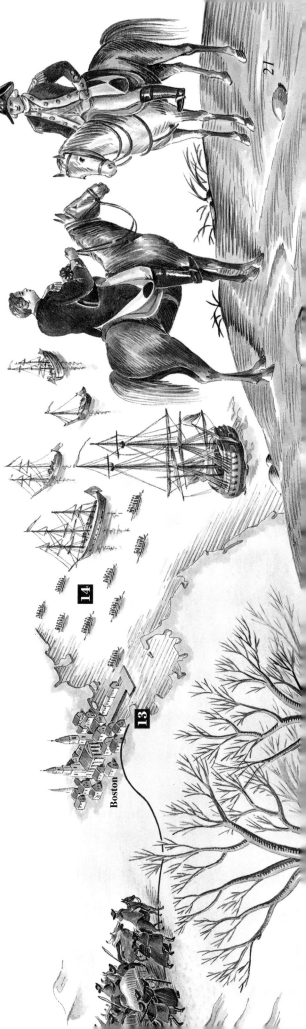

and pulled the 60 tons of artillery, loading most of it onto a wide-bottomed boat called a scow.

Leaving William in charge of sailing the artillery down Lake George, Henry went ahead with a few men in a smaller boat. The first night, they were welcomed by American Indians living at Sabbath Day Point. **2** For the next two days they struggled down the lake, rowing against the wind all day and stopping at night to warm themselves in the frigid cold. **3** At Fort George, **4** Henry Knox waited for the scow. First, bad news arrived: the scow had sunk with all of the artillery and William Knox aboard. Then good news arrived: the scow had been so near shore that the crew had saved the boat. Two days later, the scow itself arrived and the 60-ton cargo was transferred onto 82 strong sleds to be pulled by horses and oxen.

The strange caravan set out, attracting crowds of curious onlookers along the way. By Christmas Day, the sleds were inching their way through two feet of snow. Henry Knox rode ahead in a sleigh. **5** Arriving in Albany, **6** he arranged for 124 teams of horses with sleighs to help the struggling caravan. As the sleighs pulled the artillery across the frozen Mohawk River, the ice cracked and one of the largest cannons sank. Henry Knox rushed back to help recover the precious gun. **7**

By January 5, 1776, the caravan itself had reached Albany, where delighted colonists pitched in to help move the artillery across the iced-over Hudson. Almost across, the last sled broke through into the icy river. **8** When the cannon was raised from the water the next morning, it was christened "the Albany."

Oxen, horses, sleds, cannons, men—the heavy caravan moved farther south and then turned east toward Boston. Ahead lay the treacherous Berkshires. Men and oxen labored to pull the big guns up and ease them down the mountain passes. **9** In Westfield, Knox had the largest cannon, "the Old Sow," fired in celebration as enthusiastic townspeople cheered the procession onward. **10** At Springfield, Knox sent home the New York men who had helped him. **11** Then the Massachusetts men and the soldiers guided the artillery on through the mud and melting snow. **12**

Near Boston, **13** General Washington welcomed Henry Knox and his amazing caravan. Then Washington planned his strategy. On March 4, after dark, 2,000 men and 400 oxen positioned the Ticonderoga cannons to fire on Boston. When the British soldiers woke up the next morning, they were no longer in control of the city. On March 17, British troops left Boston forever. **14** Henry Knox's wild idea had paid off.

HENRY KNOX FACTS

- *The cost of Henry Knox's expedition was only about $2,500 in today's money.*
- *Henry Knox served under George Washington throughout the American Revolution, and in 1783 he succeeded him as commander of the armed forces. President Washington appointed Knox as the United States' first secretary of war.*
- *Fort Knox, where U.S. gold is stored, is named for Henry Knox.*

To the Pacific with Lewis and Clark

Gentle breezes rippled the wide Missouri River on the afternoon of May 14, 1804. Along the riverbanks, crowds cheered as 22 men rowed the long keelboat upstream against the current. Others manned the two boats called pirogues. After months of preparation, the Lewis and Clark expedition was setting out at last. The group would travel for 18 months, over thousands of difficult miles, before reaching its destination: the Pacific Ocean.

LEWIS AND CLARK

1804

The expedition began in the mind of President Thomas Jefferson. Jefferson wanted United States control over trade on the Pacific coast, and he wanted to find out everything he could about the vast Louisiana Territory. So he decided to send his secretary, Meriwether Lewis, on an expedition west to the Pacific. Lewis, in turn, asked his old army friend William Clark to command the journey with him.

Together Lewis and Clark assembled a Corps of Discovery. With extra boatmen and an interpreter, the starting expedition numbered 45 men in all. The oldest was 34, the youngest only 18. One man, York, was a slave. When they set out that May day, **1** the boats

were loaded with food, guns and ammunition, and presents for the native people along the way. Day after day the men struggled up the Missouri as it flowed across the plains. Day after day they looked for the people said to live in the area. But it was summertime, and the Plains Indians were off hunting buffalo. Finally, on August 3, the expedition met a small group of Oto and Missouri peoples. Dressed in fancy uniforms, Lewis and Clark presented gifts and a greeting from the "Great Chief the President." **2**

The Corps pushed on—collecting specimens, observing, and delivering the president's message of peace to the American Indians along the way. As winter came, the expedition stopped in the homeland of the Mandan and Hidatsa people. **3** It was a winter so cold that herds of buffalo could walk across the frozen river. When the ice broke in springtime, the Corps shoved off in two pirogues and six smaller canoes. They moved toward a world unknown to all of them except one. Traveling with them now as an interpreter was Sacagawea, a young woman from the Shoshone people in the west. **4**

Ahead lay dangers and hardships. Once Lewis barely escaped a giant grizzly bear by jumping into the water. **5** Other struggles took longer: When the Corps came to the Great Falls of the Missouri, they had to drag the boats 18 miles across land. **6**

PACIFIC OCEAN

CASCADES

Mount Hood

Columbia River

Snake River

Salmon River

ROCKY MOUNTAINS

Missouri River

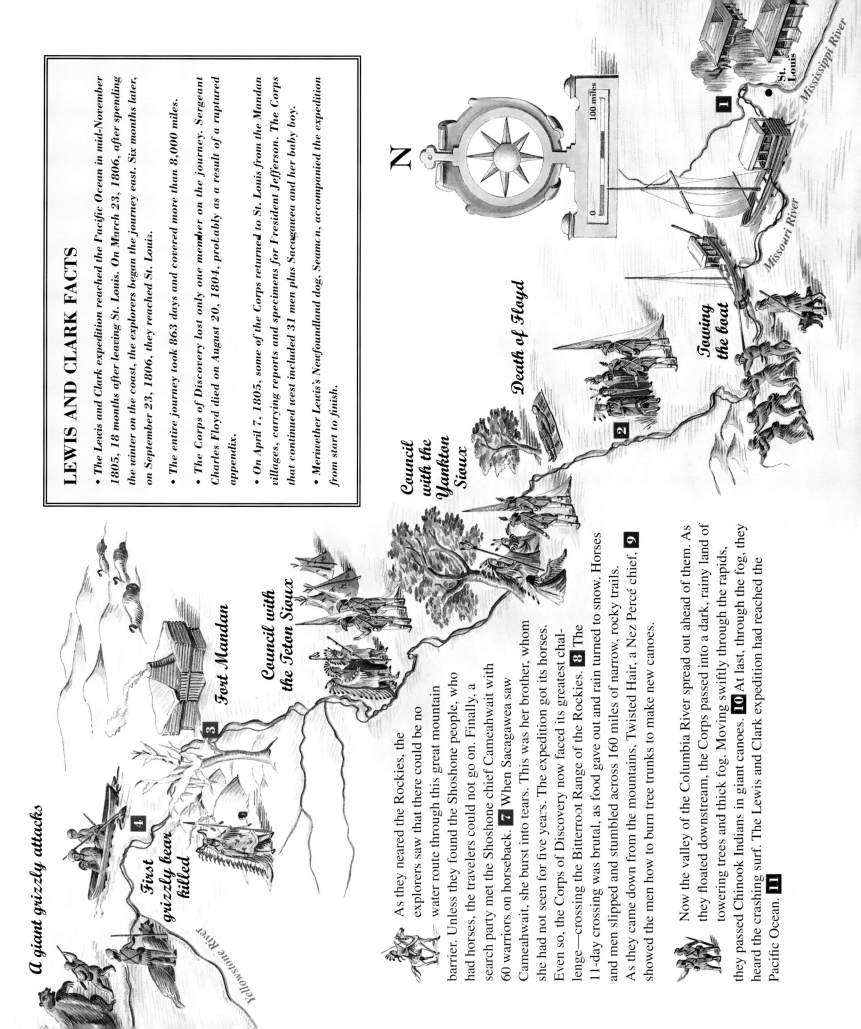

LEWIS AND CLARK FACTS

- The Lewis and Clark expedition reached the Pacific Ocean in mid-November 1805, 18 months after leaving St. Louis. On March 23, 1806, after spending the winter on the coast, the explorers began the journey east. Six months later, on September 23, 1806, they reached St. Louis.

- The entire journey took 863 days and covered more than 8,000 miles.

- The Corps of Discovery lost only one member on the journey. Sergeant Charles Floyd died on August 20, 1804, probably as a result of a ruptured appendix.

- On April 7, 1805, some of the Corps returned to St. Louis from the Mandan villages, carrying reports and specimens for President Jefferson. The Corps that continued west included 31 men plus Sacagawea and her baby boy.

- Meriwether Lewis's Newfoundland dog, Seaman, accompanied the expedition from start to finish.

A giant grizzly attacks

First grizzly bear killed

4

Yellowstone River

3

Fort Mandan

Council with the Teton Sioux

Council with the Yankton Sioux

Death of Floyd

2

Towing the boat

1

Missouri River

St. Louis

Mississippi River

N

100 miles
0

As they neared the Rockies, the explorers saw that there could be no water route through this great mountain barrier. Unless they found the Shoshone people, who had horses, the travelers could not go on. Finally, a search party met the Shoshone chief Cameahwait with 60 warriors on horseback. **7** When Sacagawea saw Cameahwait, she burst into tears. This was her brother, whom she had not seen for five years. The expedition got its horses. Even so, the Corps of Discovery now faced its greatest challenge—crossing the Bitterroot Range of the Rockies. **8** The 11-day crossing was brutal, as food gave out and rain turned to snow. Horses and men slipped and stumbled across 160 miles of narrow, rocky trails. As they came down from the mountains, Twisted Hair, a Nez Percé chief, **9** showed the men how to burn tree trunks to make new canoes.

Now the valley of the Columbia River spread out ahead of them. As they floated downstream, the Corps passed into a dark, rainy land of towering trees and thick fog. Moving swiftly through the rapids, they passed Chinook Indians in giant canoes. **10** At last, through the fog, they heard the crashing surf. The Lewis and Clark expedition had reached the Pacific Ocean. **11**

Dame Shirley Goes to the Gold Rush

San Francisco

NORTH AMERICA

Overland route

New York

Panama route

Equator

SOUTH AMERICA

ATLANTIC OCEAN

Cape Horn

0 — 1000 miles

N

LOUISE CLAPPE

1849

Louise Amelia Knapp Smith Clappe was worried. Though she loved to travel, nothing had prepared her for the 18,000-mile voyage she had just begun. Louise was sailing to California with her new husband, Dr. Fayette Clappe, in 1849. Nine months earlier, President James Polk had confirmed the wild rumors that were spreading around the world. Yes, gold had been discovered in California. Now the rush for gold was on, and 30-year-old Louise was part of it.

Louise Clappe's journey began on August 20, 1849, when the sloop *Manilla* left New York Harbor. ①₁ After several months at sea, the *Manilla* approached the dreaded Cape Horn. ②₂ where violent storms tossed ships about like twigs in a tornado. Past the danger, the *Manilla* traveled north along the western coast of South America. On January 11, 1850—almost five months after she set out—Louise Clappe sailed past the Golden Gate to the busy little town of San Francisco. ③₃

For a year and a half, the Clappes remained in San Francisco. But Fayette was often sick in the damp climate around the bay.

By September 1851 Louise and Fayette had decided to try their luck in the mining country. Fayette left first, then Louise took a small steamboat up-river to Marysville. ④₄ Enchanted by the possibility of adventure, Louise was curious about the rough mining camps she had heard so much about. And she was excited, for she had a new project. At the suggestion of a newspaper editor, she was going to write about her adventures. She had even chosen a pen name—Dame Shirley.

Louise's first California adventure was the trip itself. After stopping at a ranch near Marysville, Louise set out by mule with Fayette. She soon found herself lying in the road when her saddle

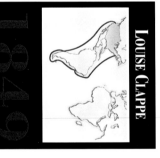

slipped. **5** She laughed, but Fayette insisted that she travel by wagon to the next stop. Louise felt as though she bounced along every stretch of the 39-mile trip to the settlement of Bidwell's Bar. **6** Sleeping arrangements at Bidwell's Bar were a tent on the flea-covered ground. So Louise and Fayette traveled on with the mules. But they got lost and had to sleep in the woods. **7** For 24 hours they tried to find their way up one path and down another. When they finally reached the Berry Creek House, Louise wanted to sleep for weeks!

The next morning, they rode to the Wild Yankee's inn, where California Indians crowded into the room to see them, **8** then on to the Buckeye Rancho. **9** Losing their way once more, they slept under the trees that night, unaware that the sounds in the distance were grizzly bears. **10**

The next day, they made their way through silent pine forests and across broad high plains. At last, looking down a great hill, Louise and Fayette could see Rich Bar, **11** the mining camp where they would live for the next few weeks. Louise galloped past a rattlesnake ready to strike and descended the treacherous trail.

Louise and Fayette settled into the Empire Hotel, the saloon and rooming house that was Rich Bar's best—and only—hotel. On September 13, 1851, Louise wrote her first letter from the gold mines. The 23 letters that Dame Shirley wrote from the mining country painted a picture of joy and sorrow, kindness and cruelty, good luck and bad. It was a life Louise Amelia Knapp Smith Clappe could not have imagined when she set sail on the *Manilla* just a few years before.

GOLD RUSH FACTS

- *Between 1848 and 1854, California produced almost $350 million worth of gold. In today's dollars the gold would be worth almost $7 billion.*

- *San Francisco grew from about 800 people in 1848 to 5,000 in 1849 and more than 20,000 in 1850.*

- *The California Indian population dropped from 150,000 in 1845 to less than 30,000 by 1870.*

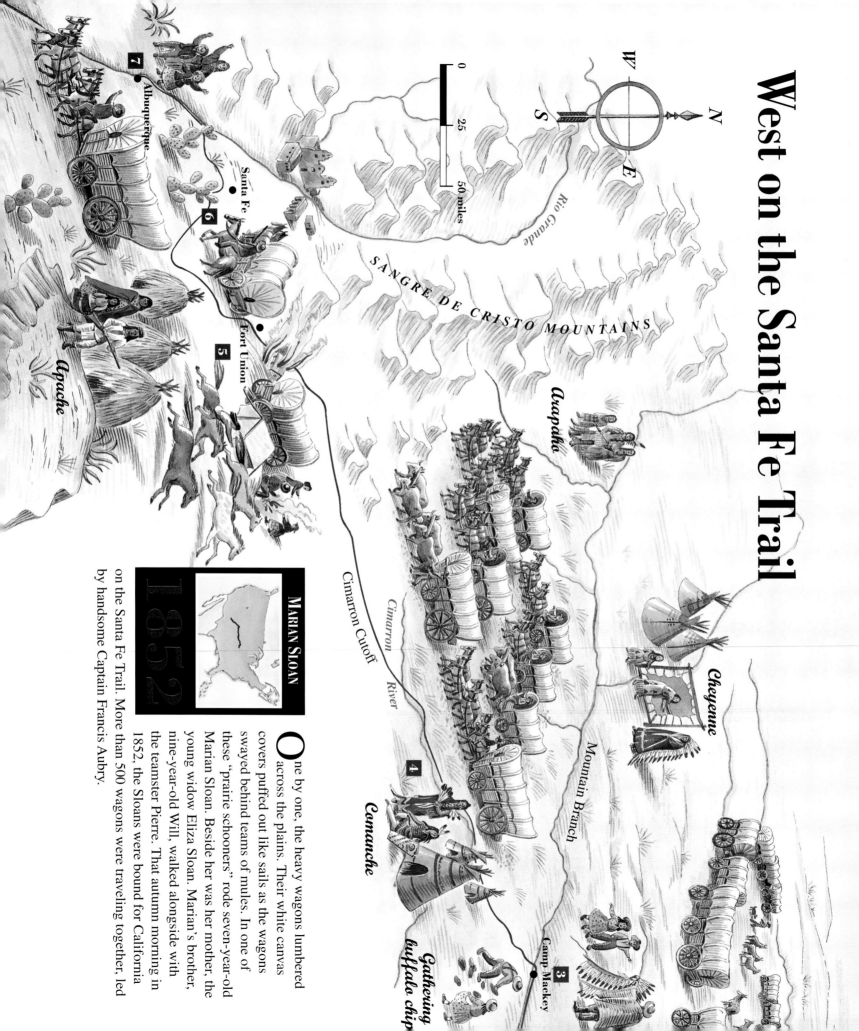

West on the Santa Fe Trail

W N E S

0   25   50 miles

Río Grande

SANGRE DE CRISTO MOUNTAINS

Arapaho

Cheyenne

Cimarron River

Mountain Branch

Cimarron Cutoff

Comanche

Gathering buffalo chips

Camp Mackey

3

4

5

Fort Union

6

Santa Fe

Albuquerque

7

Apache

MARIAN SLOAN

1852

One by one, the heavy wagons lumbered across the plains. Their white canvas covers puffed out like sails as the wagons swayed behind teams of mules. In one of these "prairie schooners" rode seven-year-old Marian Sloan. Beside her was her mother, the young widow Eliza Sloan. Marian's brother, nine-year-old Will, walked alongside with the teamster Pierre. That autumn morning in 1852, the Sloans were bound for California on the Santa Fe Trail. More than 500 wagons were traveling together, led by handsome Captain Francis Aubry.

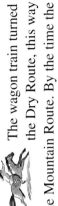

The last firewood

Hunting buffalo

Kiowa

Pawnee

● Franklin

Missouri River

Fort Leavenworth

● Independence

Santa Fe Trail

● Council Grove

Pawnee Rock **2**

Arkansas River

Since 1821 wagon trains had rolled across the plains to Santa Fe. Traders shipped goods back and forth, two to three tons of freight in a wagon. The U.S. government sent soldiers and livestock to the forts along the Santa Fe Trail. And sometimes pioneers like the Sloans went west with the freight.

"All's set!" the drivers called as the wagon train started out from Fort Leavenworth, Kansas. **1** They soon came to the route that was the Santa Fe Trail, a path of wagon ruts crossing the plains. Through tall buffalo grass, then over the shortgrass prairie, the wagon train rolled along. The land looked "like a green ocean," one traveler wrote.

When the day's journey ended, the wagons formed two great circles, with the animals and people inside. Once, when the wagon train camped at Pawnee Rock, **2** the night exploded with sound. Horses screamed. Mules stampeded. Marian and Will heard the shouts of American Indians. When dawn came, the horses were gone.

At Camp Mackey, **3** there was an Indian headdress for Captain Aubry and a protected night for the travelers. For the wagon trains, each U.S. military post was a safe haven from attack by the Pawnee, Apache, Comanche, and other peoples who had lived and hunted on the land for centuries.

The wagon train turned off on the Cimarron Cutoff. **4** Called the Dry Route, this way was shorter but more dangerous than the Mountain Route. By the time the wagons reached Fort Union, winter had set in. For weeks they camped outsice the high stockade fence of the fort. There Indians ran off with the horses once again. **5**

Finally it was time to push on. When the wagon train reached Santa Fe, **6** with its low adobe houses and broad plaza, many of the drivers set out for a return trip east. Other wagons went on with freight and with travelers like the Sloans

Along the way, however, Eliza Sloan's dream of California died. Someone stole the small basket in which she kept her money and jewelry. Unable to go on, Eliza settled in Albuquerque with Marian and Will. As Marian watched the wagon train move west without them, she thought her heart would break. **7** Marian Sloan would make five round trips on the Santa Fe Trail in her lifetime. But for now, the journey was over.

SANTA FE TRAIL FACTS

- *The Santa Fe Trail from Independence to Santa Fe was about 800 miles long. The average journey took about eight weeks.*
- *In 1852 the fare for a passenger traveling from Fort Leavenworth to Santa Fe by wagon train was $250 for adults, $125 for children. The rate for freight was $10 for 100 pounds.*
- *By 1860 trade on the Santa Fe Trail cmounted to $3.5 million (more than $53 million in current dollars).*

Big Joe Bailey Takes the Underground Railroad

JOE BAILEY

1856

It was dark when Harriet Tubman came for Big Joe Bailey. On the night of November 15, 1856, Harriet Tubman guided Joe Bailey and his brother Bill, Peter Pennington, and Eliza Nokey away from Bucktown, Maryland, where they were held in slavery. She led them away from their owners in the South and took them to freedom in the North, where slavery was against the law. **1**

For the first six days and nights, Harriet Tubman took Joe Bailey and the others through slave states—Maryland and Delaware. They were pursued from the beginning, but Harriet Tubman knew how and where to hide. She had led people north many times since her own escape in 1849. Following the North Star by night, she guided her group through woods, along roads, over fields, even into swamps. Wherever possible, she hid their tracks by walking through streams. **2** Water "never tells no tales," she said.

Sometimes hiding separately, sometimes wearing disguises, the fugitives pressed on. They walked by night and hid by day. **3** Harriet Tubman knew who would help her on the journey. A secret network of people formed an "underground railroad," an escape route from slavery. At "stations" along the way—on someone's farm, in a home, a church, or a store—brave people hid runaways.

By the time the group reached the bridge into Wilmington, there were posters all around. A reward of $1,500 was offered "to any person who will apprehend the said Joe Bailey and lodge him safely in the jail." Other posters offered $12,000 for the capture of "Moses," the mysterious person who was stealing slaves. Like Moses in the Bible, Harriet Tubman led her people to freedom.

28

CANADA 8

Lake Erie

Niagara Falls

Danger was everywhere, but Harriet Tubman knew what to do. She sent a message across the river to Thomas Garrett, a merchant known to help runaway slaves. In the morning, Garrett sent two wagons across the bridge, filled with straw and workers. That night, the wagons crossed back into Wilmington with another load: hidden under the straw were Harriet Tubman, Joe Bailey, and the others. **4**

Garrett sent the travelers on their way to Philadelphia. **5** Pennsylvania was a free state, but even there the group was not safe. The Fugitive Slave Law made it illegal for Americans anywhere to help an escaped slave. So, hiding along the way, the travelers made their way to New York. **6**

Joe Bailey had survived so far with bravery and determination. Then, in the New York Anti-Slavery Office, someone said, "Well, I'm glad to see the man whose head is worth 1500 dollars." Horrified, Joe Bailey realized that he could be recognized even in New York. He was 300 miles from safety in Canada. Could he ever make it? He sank into a deep and silent depression. **7**

On the last stretch of the journey, the fugitives traveled by train. Sometimes they hid in baggage cars. Sometimes they sat in the cars with sympathetic passengers. From New York City to Albany to Rochester, Joe Bailey never spoke. He never sang with the others.

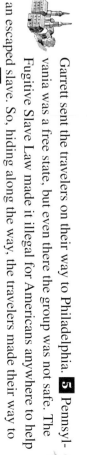

At last, they reached the river between the United States and Canada. The moment the train crossed the bridge, Harriet Tubman jumped up and grabbed Joe Bailey. "Joe, you've shook the lion's paw. Joe, you're free!" she cried. Tears streamed down Joe Bailey's face and he began to sing. **8** He sang and sang and sang. "Glory to God and Jesus too: One more soul is safe! Oh, go and carry the news; one more soul got safe!" Big Joe Bailey had taken the Underground Railroad all the way to freedom.

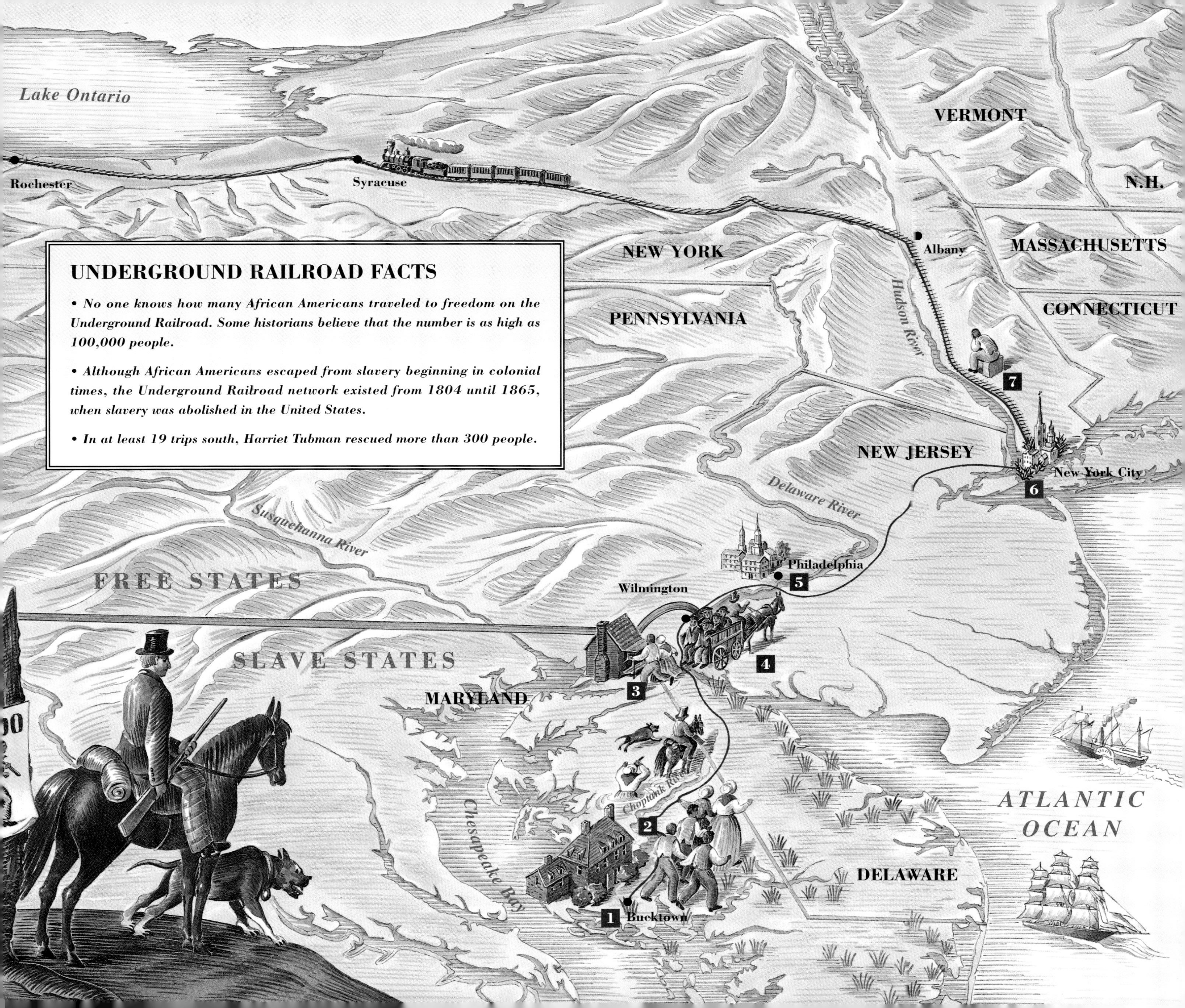

ATLANTIC OCEAN

Lake Ontario

Rochester

Syracuse

VERMONT

N.H.

MASSACHUSETTS

CONNECTICUT

New York City

6

7

Albany

Hudson River

NEW YORK

PENNSYLVANIA

NEW JERSEY

Delaware River

Philadelphia

5

4

Wilmington

3

2

1

Bucktown

DELAWARE

MARYLAND

Chesapeake Bay

Susquehanna River

FREE STATES

SLAVE STATES

UNDERGROUND RAILROAD FACTS

• No one knows how many African Americans traveled to freedom on the Underground Railroad. Some historians believe that the number is as high as 100,000 people.

• Although African Americans escaped from slavery beginning in colonial times, the Underground Railroad network existed from 1804 until 1865, when slavery was abolished in the United States.

• In at least 19 trips south, Harriet Tubman rescued more than 300 people.

A Civil War Journey

Orlando French looked over the battlefield in horror. Dead and wounded soldiers lay everywhere. In a hospital hurriedly set up on the field, a surgeon amputated the legs of men struck by cannonballs. Orlando French was the quartermaster of the 75th Illinois Volunteers, in charge of his regiment's supplies. It was October 9, 1862. Just a few days earlier, Orlando had written to his wife, Lydia. We'll beat the Rebs "in short order," he said. Now the regiment had faced its first battle. Friends were injured. Friends were dead. "Oh I tell you, it is awful, awful," he wrote to Lydia now.

Orlando French had joined the Union army a month earlier, one of 850 men who volunteered to form a regiment in Dixon, Illinois, **1** The Union and the Confederacy had been at war for 18 months now, and President Lincoln needed more soldiers.

After the battle at Perryville, Kentucky, **2** the Union soldiers marched farther south. The line of men was three miles long, with supply wagons stretched out six miles behind them. At Nashville **3** the troops stopped to prepare for the winter battles ahead. Every day Orlando French received shipments from railroads and wagons. And every day he sent soldiers out to buy or take from local people what the army needed.

At the end of December, the Union commanders moved more than 41,000 soldiers yet farther south. In a bitter battle at Murfreesboro, Tennessee, **4** they faced almost 35,000 Confederates. The battle's human cost was enormous—more than 24,000 men dead and wounded. Both sides spent the next six months recovering their strength and their supplies. Orlando did his job well and was promoted to lieutenant.

In late June the Union soldiers, now more than 60,000 strong, set out toward Chattanooga. Crossing the Cumberland Mountains with the supply wagons took days, as soldiers pushed and pulled the mules and balanced wagons with ropes. **5** On the other side,

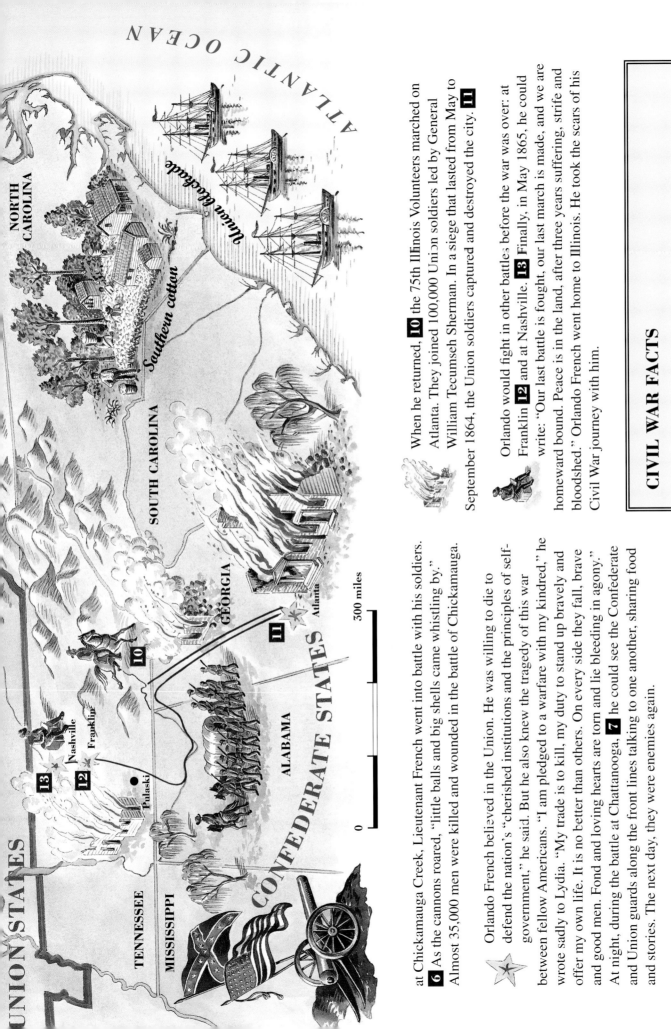

at Chickamauga Creek, Lieutenant French went into battle with his soldiers. **6** As the cannons roared, "little balls and big shells came whistling by." Almost 35,000 men were killed and wounded in the battle of Chickamauga.

Orlando French believed in the Union. He was willing to die to defend the nation's "cherished institutions and the principles of self-government," he said. But he also knew the tragedy of this war between fellow Americans. "I am pledged to a warfare with my kindred," he wrote sadly to Lydia. "My trade is to kill, my duty to stand up bravely and offer my own life. It is no better than others. On every side they fall, brave and good men. Fond and loving hearts are torn and lie bleeding in agony." At night, during the battle at Chattanooga, **7** he could see the Confederate and Union guards along the front lines talking to one another, sharing food and stories. The next day, they were enemies again.

As 1863 came to an end, Orlando prayed that the war would soon be over. But this was not to be. At the battle of Lookout Mountain **8** he was almost killed as shells screamed by his ears, struck at his feet, and passed between him and the officer standing by his side. That night, he dreamed that an Angel of Hope and Peace hovered over the battle-field. When the battle was over, the exhausted troops rested for five months and Orlando was allowed to go home for a visit. **9**

When he returned, **10** the 75th Illinois Volunteers marched on Atlanta. They joined 100,000 Union soldiers led by General William Tecumseh Sherman. In a siege that lasted from May to September 1864, the Union soldiers captured and destroyed the city. **11**

Orlando would fight in other battles before the war was over: at Franklin **12** and at Nashville. **13** Finally, in May 1865, he could write: "Our last battle is fought, our last march is made, and we are homeward bound. Peace is in the land, after three years suffering, strife and bloodshed." Orlando French went home to Illinois. He took the scars of his Civil War journey with him.

CIVIL WAR FACTS

- *The Civil War began on April 12, 1861. The final surrender of Confederate forces took place on April 26, 1865.*

- *Casualties of Union and Confederate forces included 617,528 dead and more than 375,000 wounded, the highest American casualties of any war. The 75th Illinois Volunteers lost 205 men in the war: 97 killed in battle and 108 who died from disease.*

Wild turkey

Bobcat

Mammoth Cave

Bear

Lime Key

INDIANA

Louisville

Ohio River

KENTUCKY

TENNESSEE

ALABAMA

N

100 miles

Bald eagle

Painted vulture
extinct 1800

Wood stork

FLORIDA

GEORGIA

Florida black wolf
extinct 1917

Panther

Lime Key

Snowy egret

Pelican

Fernandina Beach

Savannah

ATLANTIC OCEAN

S. CAROLINA

N. CAROLINA

Carolina parrot
extinct 1914

Heath hen
extinct 1932

Deer

Eastern bison
extinct 1825

Passenger pigeon
extinct 1890

APPALACHIAN MOUNTAINS

John Muir Walks America

JOHN MUIR

1867

John Muir was always a wanderer: "I loved to wander in the fields to hear the birds sing, and along the sea-shore to gaze and wonder," he wrote of his boyhood. Now John Muir was 29 years old, starting out on the longest walk of his life. Wherever he was, John studied the natural world around him—the birds, the flowers, the trees, everything in nature. He called this "botanizing." By 1867 John Muir had botanized all over the Midwest. He was ready to see "the warm end of the country," he said. So he set out to walk from Indiana all the way to Florida, botanizing along the way.

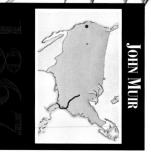

On September 2, John crossed the Ohio River from Indiana to Kentucky and began his 1,000-mile walk. Just outside Louisville, he sat down in the woods, took out his map, and planned his route. **1** He wanted "the wildest, leafiest, least trodden way" he could find.

As he walked along, John Muir looked with care and fascination at the natural world around him. Even when he lay down to sleep, John was botanizing. He noted the kinds of trees he slept under, and the birds who woke him up. **2**

Along the way, John stopped to see the famous Mammoth Cave **3** and climbed his first mountain. He took in the beauty of his first mountain stream and pronounced the surroundings the "most heavenly place I ever entered." **4** A few weeks later, though, he was caught in the current of the swift-moving Chattahoochee River. Luckily, he caught hold of a rock and hauled himself out on the overhanging vines. **5**

The natural world changed continually as John traveled farther south. By early October he had reached the cypress swamps of Georgia. **6** Surrounded by Spanish moss and other plants he had

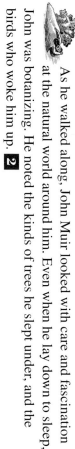

YOSEMITE NATIONAL PARK

Steller's jay

California bighorn

Coyote

Bear

Merced River

Glacier Point

Mountain lion

Deer

Mariposa Grove

N

0 5 miles

never seen before, he felt as though he were in "a strange land. I know hardly any of the plants and few of the birds." His surroundings seemed even stranger when he got to Savannah. Out of money, John slept in the Bonaventure Cemetery for five days until his brother sent funds. **7**

Next John took a small steamship, the *Sylvan Shore*, to the coast of Florida. **8** When he landed at Fernandina Beach on October 15, he found himself in another new environment. At first, he felt lonely and a little frightened. Sitting on a dry spot in the salt marsh, **9** eating his breakfast, John suddenly heard a rustling sound. Instead of the alligator John had feared, he saw a graceful bird beside him. Finally, when John Muir reached the Gulf of Mexico, his 1,000-mile walk was completed. **10** But he would spend the rest of his life in love with the natural world. In time he would become the most famous naturalist in America.

By 1903 even the president of the United States wanted to see the natural world through John Muir's eyes. When President Theodore Roosevelt came to California, he asked John Muir to show him the beautiful Sierra Nevada. In May 1903 the naturalist and the president spent three days together in the Yosemite Valley. People were shocked when the president of the United States camped out with only a blanket, first in Mariposa Grove, **11** then at Glacier Point. **12** By the trip's end, **13** John Muir had convinced the president to protect the Yosemite Valley from development. Together they had done "something for wildness and to make the mountains glad."

Thirty-six years earlier, John Muir's 1,000-mile walk had taught him that only "by going alone in silence, without baggage, can one truly get into the heart of the wilderness." For the rest of his life, he helped presidents and ordinary people find the heart of the natural world.

JOHN MUIR FACTS

- *John Muir was born in Scotland in 1838. He came to the United States with his family when he was 11 years old.*

- *In 1892 John Muir founded the Sierra Club to help protect the environment. Today the club has more than 600,000 members.*

- *In 1903 there were 8 parks in the new National Park system. Today there are 54 national parks.*

Drag rider

Drag rider

Flank rider

Swing rider

Rio Grande

Remuda

Wrangler

Mealtime

Coyotes

Gulf of Mexico

Victoria

TEXAS

NEW MEXICO

COLORADO

ROCKY MOUNTAINS

WYOMING TERRITORY

Red River

Fort Worth

INDIAN TERRITORY

Dodge City

KANSAS

NEBR.

South Platte River

Atchinson, Topeka & Santa Fe R.R.

Chicago

1 2 3 4 5 6 7 8 9 10

A Cowboy's Journey

When the trail boss waved his hat, the cowboys started the cattle north up the Chisholm Trail. "Ho cattle, ho!" they cried as Tom Snyder's herd of 2,000 Texas longhorns began their four-month walk from Texas to Wyoming. Riding with them was Baylis John Fletcher, a 19-year-old Texan looking for adventure. Fletcher had "trail fever," he said, and he wanted to take a cowboy's journey.

All through the 1860s and 1870s, cattle drives moved millions of animals from Texas ranches to Kansas towns. There the cattle were sent by railroad to meatpacking centers in the Midwest and East. The long, hard trip was worth it. A cow selling for $4 in Texas could bring $40 in Chicago. By 1879 the network of cattle trails and railroad lines had created a northern ranching business in states like Wyoming.

Baylis Fletcher's adventure began on a ranch near Victoria, Texas. **1** After a month of rounding up and branding the herd, the trail outfit started the drive on April 11, 1879. Led by trail boss George Arnett, the outfit included Fletcher, seven other cowboys, and Manuel García, the cook. There was also a horse wrangler in charge of the remuda, the herd of 80 horses the cowboys would ride.

The herd moved in a cloud of dust—a noisy crowd of steers, cows, calves, and horses. Always following the lead steer, the herd spread out sometimes 50 feet wide, sometimes only 10. Cowboys rode in front, back, and alongside, patrolling to keep the herd together and to keep the animals from stampeding—the great danger of a cattle drive. Any sudden sound could spook the nervous longhorns, sending panicked animals in all directions. Then cowboys risked their lives to bring the herd under control. One night, Baylis Fletcher was in the saddle from midnight to dawn

when the herd stampeded near Spring Creek. **2** Near Gonzalez a few days later, Baylis rounded up the bellowing cattle on his favorite horse, Happy Jack. He lost his hat but stayed in the saddle. **3** Hail caused a stampede at Salado Creek, **4** and coyotes caused one at Steele's Creek. **5**

In the growing town of Fort Worth, **6** the outfit stocked up on supplies, the last chance for 500 miles. By June 1, the men could see the Red River Valley and Indian Territory. Crossing the river at Spanish Fort, the chuck wagon, carrying the cook and all of the food, had to be rescued from quicksand. **7** Soon there was good luck, however—grass so rich the animals could graze as they walked.

Just after July 4, the drive reached Dodge City. **8** Deputy marshals Bat Masterson and Wyatt Earp tried to control the town's crime, but many said it was "the wickedest town in the West." Baylis didn't have much chance to find out, though. The trail boss moved the cowboys on through western Kansas as soon as he could.

When the herd crossed the muddy South Platte River, Baylis remembered that people said it was "too thick to drink and too thin to plow." **9** In Wyoming Territory, the cattle drive reached a high plateau where Baylis feasted his eyes on "the backbone of America." A few days later the cattle were delivered to the Horse Creek ranch. **10** Wages in their pockets and new clothes on their backs, the trail outfit disbanded. Baylis Fletcher went home with his stories. When he told them, he knew "I should never regret having made a drive up the old Chisholm Trail."

CATTLE DRIVE FACTS

- *Between 9 and 10 million cattle moved out of Texas on cattle drives from the late 1860s to the early 1880s. On a drive, cattle averaged about 12 miles a day.*

- *Longhorns descended from Spanish cattle brought by Columbus and other explorers.*

- *Cowboys named the Chisholm Trail in honor of Jesse Chisholm, a trader and guide.*

Point rider   Chuck wagon   Trail boss

Rosa Cristoforo Comes to America

1884

R osa Cristoforo clutched little Francesco as she said goodbye. Heartbroken, she kissed her baby son's eyes and his cheeks and his lips. Then she gave him to her mother and left for America. Sixteen-year-old Rosa did not want to leave her family and her friends and her village in Lombardy, in the north of Italy. And she did not want to cross the ocean to a country that she did not know, to be with a husband whom she did not love.

A year earlier Rosa's husband, Santino, had left Bugiarno for America. With other men from the village, he was hired to work in the iron mines of Missouri. Rosa, whose mother had forced her to marry the older man, was glad when he went away. But now one of the men who went with Santino had come back to the village. The men in America wanted their wives, and they sent Pep to get them. When the word came, Rosa's mother said that she must go to her husband. 'But you must leave the baby with me,' she demanded. 'I will be too lonely without him.' So Rosa did as her mother said.

By the church in the village square, she got on the horse-drawn bus to start her trip to America. **1** Then Rosa boarded a train with Pep and the others from Bugiarno. **2** America seemed far away and frightening. "Don't be so sad," friends said. "You will get smart in America. And in America you will not be so poor." Rosa and her *paesani*—the people from her homeland—traveled first to Paris **3** and then on to the port of Le Havre. **4** Le Havre was crowded with immigrants wanting to board the ships to America. For days Pep tried to get his little group onto a ship, but all were full. Finally they found space on a vessel bound for New York.

The *paesani* from Bugiarno were crowded in belowdecks with the other poor people traveling in third class, called steerage. Men, women, and children shared one dark, airless room. At night they slept side by side on wooden shelves. During the day, when they walked on the small steerage deck, Rosa could hear the sounds of Europe all around her: the chatter of immigrants from France, Germany, Sweden, Italy. Four days out to sea, the chatter turned to moans when a great storm came up. **5** Steerage passengers were closed in belowdecks for three days, with no light or fresh air, while the ship tossed in the battering waves. "We were like rats trapped in a hole," Rosa said. There was no need to worry about seeing Santino, she thought. She was sure to drown instead.

Days later, the ship reached New York Harbor. **6** Silently, Rosa stood on the deck. All the passengers had on their best clothes, their belongings wrapped in bundles beside them. As the ship sailed into the bay, seagulls shrieked, bands played, flags waved. But Rosa and her *paesani* were quiet. Suddenly America was real—with all that they dreamed of and all that they feared.

The mines

MISSOURI
Union

St. Louis

10 **9**

8

ILLINOIS INDIANA OHIO

PENNSYLVANIA

NEW YORK

N.J.
6
New York City
7

A T L A N T I C   O C E A N

Map labels: AUSTRO-HUNGARIAN EMPIRE · ITALY · GERMAN EMPIRE · FRANCE · UNITED KINGDOM · Paris · Le Havre · *Mediterranean Sea* · ATLANTIC OCEAN

IMMIGRATION FACTS

- *In 1884—the year Rosa Cristoforo arrived—518,592 people immigrated to the United States.*

- *Between 1876 and 1926 almost 9 million people emigrated from Italy to the Americas. About 300,000 Italians came to the United States in the 1880s.*

- *From 1855 to 1892 (when Ellis Island opened) immigrants in steerage were processed through Castle Garden when they arrived in New York.*

- *Most immigrants were admitted to the United States on the day they arrived. Only about 2 percent were sent back to their homelands.*

Before Rosa and the others could step foot in America, there were tests to pass. In the harbor, doctors boarded the boat to check the immigrants' eyes and their vaccination records.

Those who passed inspection could go on to Castle Garden, the building where immigrants like Rosa were admitted to the United States. [7] "What is your name? Where do you come from? Where are you going?" officials demanded. Finally, Rosa heard the call "Cristoforo, Rosa." One by one Rosa and her companions passed through a door into the United States.

As Pep led the young women out, a smooth-talking stranger called to him in Italian. Introducing himself as a country-man—Signore Bartini—the man welcomed his *paesani* to America. 'There are no trains to Missouri for three days,' he lied, 'so you will need to stay in my hotel.' As he had done to hundreds of immigrants before, Bartini cheated Pep and the young women out of all the money they had. And then he put them on a train to Missouri. [8]

Now Rosa and her *paesani* had a trip of several days ahead of them, with no money to buy food. By the time they reached St. Louis, [9] though, excitement had overtaken hunger. Some of the young women wanted to see their husbands, but Rosa prayed. Santino had been a mean husband and she feared what he would be like in America.

When the train arrived in Union, Missouri, [10] two wagons of *paesani* from Lombardy were there to meet it. As everyone hugged and laughed and cried, Rosa could see Santino standing apart. Santino did not smile, nor did he come to greet her. He just stared. Trying to calm herself, Rosa piled into a wagon with the others and set out for the mines. When they arrived, the newcomers fell silent as they saw their new lives ahead of them. Tired miners were pushing wheelbarrows. The shacks where they lived lay on land bare of grass or trees. America, the Promised Land, looked very bleak.

In the years to come, Rosa would make a new life for herself. She would leave the cruel Santino and marry again. She would bring her young son, Francesco, to America, and she would have other children. She would be proud that she was an American. "That's what I learned in America," Rosa would say: "not to be afraid."

Coast to Coast in the VIN FIZ

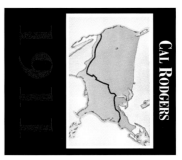

CAL RODGERS

Cal Rodgers was very brave, and he was very determined. On a beautiful Sunday afternoon—September 17, 1911—he stood proudly beside his brand-new airplane, the *Vin Fiz*. Cal Rodgers wanted to set a record and win a prize. To set the record he needed to be the first to fly from coast to coast across the United States. To win the $50,000 prize, he needed to do it in 30 days. The makers of Vin Fiz, a new soft drink, offered to pay Cal's expenses. They also provided a train to follow his path. The train would carry spare parts and a team of mechanics. All would be needed!

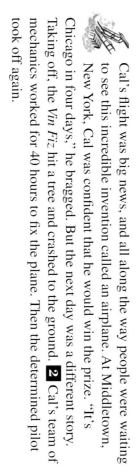

Cal Rodgers set off that Sunday afternoon from Sheepshead Bay, on the Atlantic Ocean in New York City. **1** His spirits were high as he flew over New York, dropping Vin Fiz ads from the air. Airplanes were a new invention in those days, and the *Vin Fiz* was the first airplane to fly over Manhattan. Flying the plane was pretty simple, since only two levers controlled all of its movements. Cal sat on a hard seat in the open plane, with no cabin, not even a windshield in front of him.

Cal's flight was big news, and all along the way people were waiting to see this incredible invention called an airplane. At Middletown, New York, Cal was confident that he would win the prize. "It's Chicago in four days," he bragged. But the next day was a different story. Taking off, the *Vin Fiz* hit a tree and crashed to the ground. **2** Cal's team of mechanics worked for 40 hours to fix the plane. Then the determined pilot took off again.

Flying by day and landing for the night, Cal felt he was "going faster than the wind." There were close calls almost every day: Parts of the plane fell off; Cal ran the *Vin Fiz* into wires; the engine failed, sometimes in midair. In Indiana, Cal found himself in the middle of a fierce thunderstorm. **3** "I didn't know what lightning might do to an aeroplane, but I didn't like the idea," Cal said later. He landed wet but safe. The next day, however, the *Vin Fiz* ran into a hill as Cal took off. Another crash, another big repair. **4**

Cal flew on, in spite of it all. By the time he reached Chicago, it was clear that he wasn't going to make it across the country in 30 days. "I'm going to do this whether I get $50,000 or 50 cents or nothing," he said. "I am going to cross this continent simply to be the first." At stop after stop, people gathered to cheer him on. On the way to Dallas, an eagle flew at the plane. But Cal landed safely, in front of 75,000 people.

The next day, the *Vin Fiz*'s engine stopped in midair, and Cal glided down to a farmer's field. **6** A few days later, the plane crashed as Cal was taking off.

7 Though the *Vin Fiz* was almost destroyed, the mechanics had it ready to go in just 24 hours. There were more accidents ahead. On November 3 part of the plane's engine exploded. **8** A few days later, loose spark plugs and a leaky radiator forced him down.

CALIFORNIA

Finally, on November 5—49 days after leaving New York—Cal Rodgers and the *Vin Fiz* reached Pasadena, the official destination. **9** When the plane landed, 10,000 cheering fans rushed up to the plane. They wrapped Cal in an American flag. He was their hero, the first man to fly across the nation.

Cal wasn't finished, though. He wanted his plane to touch the Pacific Ocean. So the next day he set out to fly the few miles from Pasadena to Long Beach. It should have been easy, but once again, the *Vin Fiz* crashed. This time, Cal was seriously injured. **10** It was more than a month before Cal was again able to fly the *Vin Fiz*. On December 10, 84 days after setting out, Cal rolled the wheels of his plane into the waters of the Pacific. **11** As 50,000 people cheered, Cal Rodgers completed his record-setting journey.

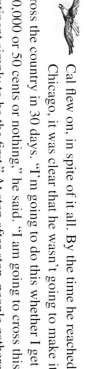

PACIFIC OCEAN

Long Beach

Pasadena

CALIFORNIA

VIN FIZ FACTS

• In 1903 Wilbur and Orville Wright made the world's first airplane flight in a 650-pound plane named Flyer.

• The Vin Fiz weighed 850 pounds, with a span of 32 feet from wingtip to wingtip.

• The trip from New York to Pasadena took 49 days, but the Vin Fiz was in the air only three days, ten hours, and four minutes.

Christening the airplane

First flight over Manhattan's "skyscrapers"

ATLANTIC OCEAN

Gulf of Mexico

MEXICO

NEW YORK

N.J.

New York

PENNSYLVANIA

OHIO

INDIANA

ILLINOIS

Chicago

MISSOURI

KANSAS

Kansas City

OKLAHOMA

TEXAS

Dallas

Fort Worth

San Antonio

NEW MEXICO

El Paso

0   200   400 miles

Louis Armstrong Heads North

LOUIS ARMSTRONG

1922

Music filled the streets as Louis Armstrong and the Tuxedo Brass Band marched back from a funeral. In the New Orleans way, the band had played sad tunes as the mourners marched to the cemetery. Now they played happy songs on the way back. It was a hot summer day, and the thirsty musicians were ready to quit. Suddenly a Western Union messenger rushed up with a telegram for Louis. It was from his idol, the jazz musician Papa Joe Oliver, who had left New Orleans for Chicago. Now he asked 21-year-old Louis to join his jazz band. Right away, Louis made up his mind to go.

Playing one last song for the funeral, Louis made the hymn "Free As a Bird" sound as if the music were smiling. Then he packed his clothes and rushed to the train station. There to send him off were the whole Tuxedo Brass Band, neighbors, and family. "It seemed like all of New Orleans had gathered at the train to give me a little luck," Louis wrote later. The black porters and waiters working on the trains wished him well, too. "Yeah, man, I'm going up to Chicago to play with my idol, Papa Joe!" Louis said, beaming his great big smile.

When the 7:00 P.M. Illinois Central pulled out of New Orleans, **1** Louis Armstrong was on his way to fame. He didn't know it, though. What mattered most to him at that point was fried chicken. On trains in those days African Americans were segregated in special cars, and there were no dining cars where they could eat. Louis's mother, Mayann Armstrong, had made him a big fish sandwich for the trip. (She had insisted that he wear his long underwear, too, so he wouldn't catch cold when he got "up north.") Once on the train, though, Louis sat down next to a woman who had a large basket of fried chicken. That chicken looked so delicious that Louis spent the next few hours figuring out how he could share it. Pretty soon his charm won over the lady and her three children, and Louis had his fill of fried chicken.

While the train click-clacked along the tracks, passing small towns and country juke joints, **2** Louis Armstrong had plenty of time to think about this big move. Except for several summers playing on a Mississippi riverboat, Louis had spent his whole life in New Orleans. Tucked into a curve of the Mississippi River, New Orleans was a sleepy city in 1922. Chicago, on the other hand, was big and brash, a whole new world.

When the train crossed the Ohio River at Cairo, Illinois, **3** Louis Armstrong joined the great black migration out of the South. Thousands of African Americans were going north seeking better opportunities, among them musicians like Joe Oliver, Jelly Roll Morton, and now Louis Armstrong.

Finally, Louis heard the train conductor call "All out for Chicago. Last stop." **4** Looking out the window at the city's tall buildings, he felt like a country boy. At the Illinois Central Station all the friends he had made on the trip streamed out of the train, greeted by relatives and friends. Louis looked up and down the platform, hoping to see Papa Joe Oliver, but the bandleader wasn't there. Feeling lonely and a little lost, he stood in the big waiting room with his small bag and his cornet case. He wondered if the trip had been such a good idea after all. But then a redcap who worked at the station approached. He asked Louis if he were the young man coming to join King Oliver's band. "King Oliver," Papa Joe was called now. Louis was impressed. Oliver had been there to meet an earlier train, the man explained. He had left instructions for Louis to be sent by taxi to Lincoln Gardens, the dance hall where the band was playing.

When Louis opened the door of Lincoln Gardens, the music poured out. At first he wondered whether he was good enough to play with the great King Oliver. But when Oliver and the other musicians jumped up to greet him, Louis knew it would all be fine. The next night Louis Armstrong played with King Oliver's Creole Jazz Band for the first time. "It was better than all the moments I'd ever had," he said.

N. Y.
W. C. Handy

GEORGIA

Bessie Smith

Ohio River

TENNESSEE

Chicago

4

ILL.

3

Cairo

MOORE'S CAFE

2

Blind Lemon Jefferson

King Oliver's Band

Mississippi River

MISSOURI

ARK.

MISS.

1

LOUISIANA   New Orleans

Gulf of Mexico

Coleman Hawkins

KANSAS

Jelly Roll Morton

COLORADO

LOUIS ARMSTRONG FACTS

- Louis Armstrong, sometimes called the "true King of Jazz," played the cornet and then the trumpet for more than 50 years. He made more than 500 recordings, appeared in 36 movies, and toured the world with his bands.

- Between 1914 and 1920 as many as 500,000 African Americans migrated to northern cities from the South. By 1922 Chicago's African American population was more than 100,000, one of the world's largest black communities.

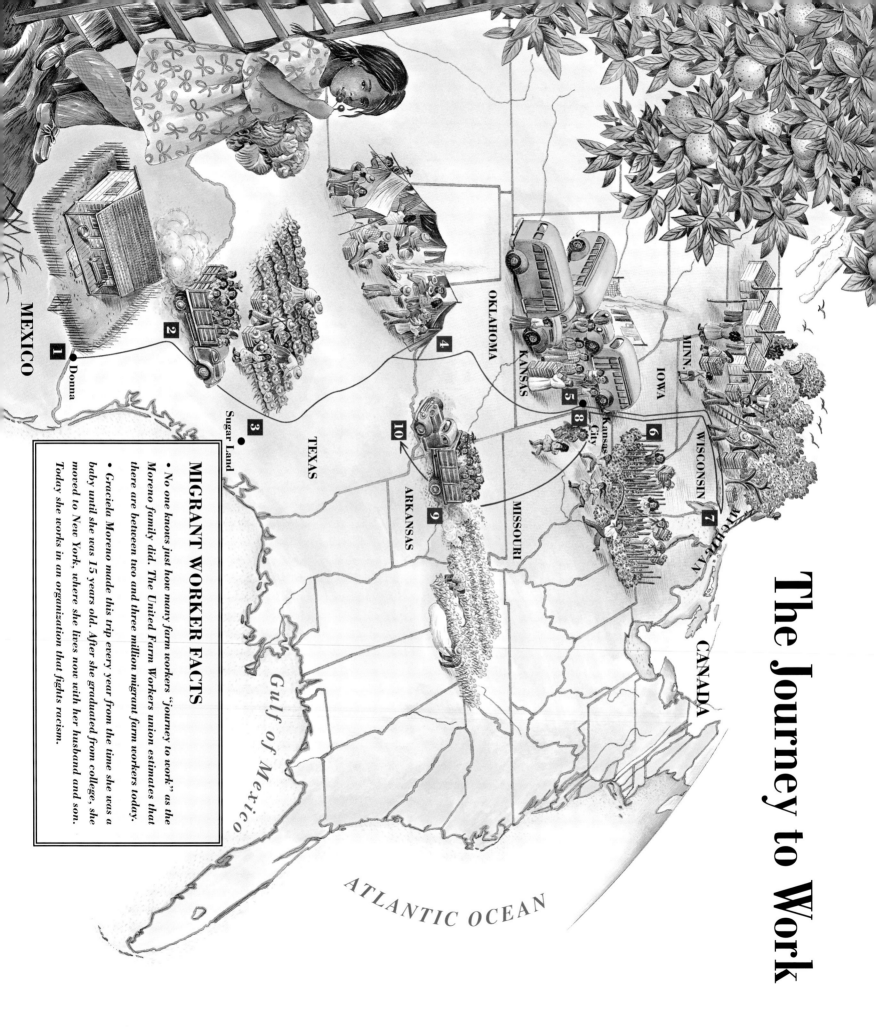

The Journey to Work

MIGRANT WORKER FACTS

- *No one knows just how many farm workers "journey to work" as the Moreno family did. The United Farm Workers union estimates that there are between two and three million migrant farm workers today.*

- *Graciela Moreno made this trip every year from the time she was a baby until she was 15 years old. After she graduated from college, she moved to New York, where she lives now with her husband and son. Today she works in an organization that fights racism.*

MEXICO

• Donna **1**

2

Sugar Land • **3**

TEXAS

Gulf of Mexico

OKLAHOMA

4

KANSAS

5

Kansas City • **8**

MISSOURI

ARKANSAS **9**

10

IOWA

6

MINN.

WISCONSIN **7**

MICHIGAN

CANADA

ATLANTIC OCEAN

GRACIELA MORENO

1959

All through the hot night, Graciela Moreno thought about the six months ahead of her. The sounds and smells of cooking drifted through the little house in Donna, Texas. Graciela heard her grandmother in the kitchen, preparing tacos for the trip. Before the first light of day, the Moreno family would set off on a 3,700-mile journey. The Morenos were farm workers. From May to October they would pick vegetables and fruit across America.

Early that May morning, the Moreno family left home. **1** They traveled in a big flatbed truck **2** with other workers from Donna—40 people in all. Ten-year-old Graciela and her little brother, Guillermo, laughed and played with the other children on the huge pile of sacks and bedrolls in the center of the truck. Mama Minga, their grandmother, was tired. She had been up all night getting ready for this trip. María Ester, their mother, was quietly unhappy. She wanted another life for herself and her children. Like most of the other adults, Uncle Rubén and his wife, Isabél, were resigned to the hard work ahead. They knew that it was the only way to support their family.

The Contractor, the man who had organized the trip, drove the truck up to Sugar Land, Texas, that first day. **3** At dawn the next morning everyone went to the fields, where long rows of green lettuce waited to be picked. Families worked together as a team. Mama Minga, María Ester, and Isabél bent low over the plants, quickly cutting each head of lettuce with their knives. Graciela and Guillermo followed behind, placing the heads carefully in boxes as fast as they could. The minute a box was filled, Uncle Rubén raced it to the end of the field. Cutting, placing, racing—the exhausting work went on from sunrise to sunset. At the end of the day, a count was taken. The farmer paid the Contractor for each box, and the Contractor paid each family. Mama Minga placed her family's money in a little bag pinned to her slip.

After a few weeks, the Contractor drove his truckload of workers up to Oklahoma. **4** As the adults set up camp in canvas lean-tos and brought water from the well, Graciela gathered wood for the fire. Over the next few weeks, they picked lettuce, cucumbers, beans, and peas. By late June they had moved on to Kansas. Graciela felt strange sleeping in the yellow school buses the farmers provided. **5** But she loved to sit outside by the fire at night, listening to the stories Mama Minga told about life in Mexico. And always, the days were filled with work, six days a week. Sunday was a day for rest and play, for the farm workers rarely felt comfortable in the local churches. In Kansas, though, a priest came to the fields to say prayers and sometimes Mass.

As summer on the Plains grew hotter and hotter, the Contractor took the farm workers north to Iowa. By now the tomatoes were ready for picking. The plants stung and scratched the workers' hands. And everyone hated the pesticides some farmers sprayed on the fields. Some days the smell was so bad that the farm workers pulled their bandanas up over their faces. Then Graciela and the other children liked to play "banditos." Mama Minga let them play now and then. But one day the farm foreman picked up a heavy stick and threatened to hit the noisy children. **6** Mama Minga stood up from her picking, and all work ceased. As the workers stared silently at the angry man, he walked away. Graciela never forgot the power of her grandmother's brave act.

By August Graciela was in Michigan, where cherries and apples were ripening on the trees. **7** The Morenos were far from home, isolated in a world that did not welcome them. Kansas was different, though. By late August they were back there to pick corn and other vegetables. At night when they weren't working, the Morenos visited their friends in "Little Donna." It felt like home, because so many farm workers from Donna had stayed to work in the canneries. There were even dances with Mexican music. **8**

In September, when other children were starting school, Graciela was picking cotton in Arkansas. **9** Cotton was the hardest crop to pick. Graciela tried not to listen when Guillermo complained about his sore hands. "Look at Mama Minga," she said. "She can pick more than one hundred pounds a day."

As the nights grew cooler, in early October, they started the drive home to Donna. **10** After six months away, Graciela was soon back at home, back at school, back in a different world . . . until next year.

Leaving Vietnam

NORTH VIETNAM

THAILAND

CAMBODIA

LAOS

CHINA

SOUTH VIETNAM

Pirates

South China Sea

Mekong Delta

Coast Guard

Kuala Lumpur

MALAYSIA

Ca Mau

Caibe

Da Nang

PHONG BUI

1976

The boy listened desperately for the sound of the helicopter coming to rescue his family. It was April 1975, and the war in Vietnam was ending. Eleven-year-old Bui Huu Phong could hear the chaos outside his home as people fled the city of Da Nang. With Communist troops approaching, helicopters were rushing the last Americans to ships that waited offshore. The Americans tried to take with them some Vietnamese like the Bui family, anti-Communists who had worked closely with the United States. Phong and his family were afraid they would be punished or even killed if they did not escape. But the helicopter coming for the Buis never arrived. Four hard years would pass before they could leave Vietnam.

After the Communists took over Da Nang, the Buis lived in fear. The new government declared successful business people like Phong's father "enemies of the working people." Finally, in 1976, the government decided to send the Buis to the countryside. There they would be "reeducated" to live like farmers. Early one morning the Bui family—mother, father, six children, and a cousin—were put on a military truck with just a few belongings. As they pulled out of Da Nang, Phong left his friends, his home, and his old life forever. **1**

The truck traveled slowly through the war-torn country. **2** It took a week to reach the tiny village of Caibe, deep in the rice fields of the Mekong Delta. **3** There Phong and his family were left alone in a bamboo forest. In shock, they faced a new life with none of the freedom or comforts they had known before. They had no house and no idea how to clear the land or grow rice. First the Buis built a shelter from what they could find: bamboo, hay, tin, and clay. Gradually they learned how to grow rice in the fields and catch fish from the nearby pond.

For three years, Phong's mother plotted the family's escape. First Phong's older brother, Hai, left on his own. Then Phong's mother arranged for the rest of the family to escape with a group of Chinese people who also were fleeing Vietnam. They were going to Malaysia, where the United Nations was helping Vietnamese refugees. Dressed in Chinese clothing, with fake IDs, Phong and the others slipped away from Caibe one night. In the coastal village of Ca Mau, they boarded a small fishing boat with 80 other refugees and headed across the South China Sea. **4**

The first days at sea were the most dangerous, as the boat avoided pirates from Thailand and patrol boats from the Vietnamese Coast Guard. All day long the refugees hid belowdecks, packed together like sardines. The adults were quiet and worried, knowing the consequences of being caught. But to teenage Phong the trip felt like an adventure. After five days, the crowded little boat reached the coast of Malaysia. There, within sight of land, it was caught on the sand and rocks. As the surf threatened to break up the vessel, Phong and two other boys swam to shore to get help. Quickly, local police went out in small boats to save the frantic passengers.

Once on shore, the exhausted refugees found that they had not reached safety after all. Swiftly and cruelly, the Malaysian police encircled them in a barbed-wire enclo- **5** sure as they stood on the beach. Phong knew then that this adventure could have a terrifying ending. He had heard grim stories of refugees killed by their rescuers. Now their only hope was to get word to Phong's aunt, Sung Fleming, who was married to an American diplomat in Bangkok. Each day Phong and his family pleaded with the villagers who watched them in their barbed-wire prison. With the last of their money, they tried to pay the villagers to send telegrams to Sung Fleming. But nothing happened. After six weeks, the refugees were still on the beach, and they were in despair.

Then one night a young village girl sneaked past the guards and barbed wire to find Phong. Using sign language, she told him that the refugees were to be sent out to sea the next day without food or water. She asked Phong to write a telegram and promised to send it to his aunt. The next day the atmosphere on the beach was tense as the Malaysian police lined up the refugees. Suddenly Phong heard the sound of a helicopter. Moments later, his aunt and a United Nations official rushed up to the barbed-wire enclosure. Released from their prison on the sand, Phong and his family embraced Sung Fleming, crying and laughing in joyous relief. Phong's little Malaysian friend had saved everyone. Within an hour, all of the refugees were taken to United Nations camps nearby. **6**

In the camps, UN officials helped them make the complicated arrangements for their new lives. When the Buis arrived at the last camp, Phong heard an excited shout. Of the thousands of refugees there, one was his brother Hai, who had fled Vietnam earlier. Reunited, the Bui family waited for word that they could come to America.

At last permission was granted and a UN official took them to Kuala Lumpur. There they spent the night in a church with 60 other refugees, playing Beatles songs and celebrating their departure. The next morning Phong and his family boarded the plane for America. **7** When they landed in Philadelphia, **8** the family was welcomed by relatives who had come to the United States before them. In America, Phong set out on a journey once again—the journey to rebuild his life, the journey to discover his new country.

VIETNAM FACTS

• *It is estimated that half of the refugees who fled Vietnam by boat never reached land again. They drowned or were killed by pirates. Of those who reached Asian refugee camps, many were sent back out to sea.*

• *The United States was directly involved in the Vietnam War from 1964 to 1975.*

• *By 1980 about 180,000 Vietnamese people had resettled in the United States.*

• *Today Bui Huu Phong is an artist living in Brooklyn, New York.*

8 Philadelphia

San Francisco

Acknowledgments

Creating this book has been a partnership from the beginning: first between its authors, who have shared this dream for a decade, and then with its illustrator, Rodica Prato, who has made this even better than our dreams. Rodica Prato can render a world in tiny pictures, with an extraordinary sense of beauty and a deep respect for the viewer. We thank her for being our partner.

Journeys in Time and *Places in Time* would not exist without the talent, dedication, and friendship of their designer, Kevin Ullrich.

The authors wish to thank Amy Flynn for her very thoughtful editing, Bob Kosturko for his talented art direction, and both for holding on to their faith in our idea.

This project would not have been realized without the generous help of Bill Smith and Bill Smith Studios, Ella Hanna, Betty Mintz, Elaine Grove, and Bennett Moe.

To tell these stories we have relied on the expertise that historians, archivists, curators, and librarians around the country have most generously shared with us. In addition to the women and men acknowledged here, we are grateful to the generations of historians whose wisdom we have tapped and to the libraries where we have found it (especially to the Bobst Library at New York University, the New York Public Library, and the New York Society Library).

Elspeth Leacock
Susan Buckley

Notes

Every journey and every person in this book is real. We found the stories in many places: in books, in manuscripts, in letters saved by a family, and sometimes by talking to the travelers themselves. Through our research we found out where and how the journeys were made. And sometimes we know exactly what people said along the way. Then we have used conventional quotation marks for dialogue. At other times we have a good idea about what people said, but we do not have historical evidence. Then we have used single quotation marks.

HOW THE ANISHINABE FOUND A NEW HOME

This journey is based on Red Sky's migration scroll. Red Sky was an Ojibwa spiritual leader, and the scroll is a picture map that was drawn on birch bark sometime in the 1800s. The map shows the ancient legend of the migration of the Anishinabe people. Thanks to Clinton Elliott, Ojibwa Resource Center, National Museum of the American Indian.

SHIP'S BOY WITH CHRISTOPHER COLUMBUS

We have based this journey on Bartolomé de las Casas's version of the logs written by Columbus. (The original logs were lost.) When counting the days at sea, we begin, as historians traditionally do, with the departure from the Canary Islands (not from Palos, where the journey begins.) The landfall island is not really known. Many believe it to be San Salvador, as we have shown. Others think it might have been Samana Cay or even Guanahani.

FOUNDING NEW MEXICO

Many of the details about Oñate and his journey were recorded in verse by Gaspar Villagrá in his *History of New Mexico*, first published in 1610. Juan de Oñate also recorded the journey in his *Itinerario*, as well as in letters. Thanks to Dr. Donald C. Cutter, Professor of History Emeritus, University of New Mexico.

THE VOYAGE OF THE MAYFLOWER

The details in this story and map are based on the journal of William Bradford, who wrote a day-by-day account of the voyage. Thanks to James Baker, Senior Historian, and the staff of Plimoth Plantation, Plymouth, Massachusetts.

BEN FRANKLIN GOES TO PHILADELPHIA

Benjamin Franklin provided the details of this journey in his autobiography. He wrote about this journey as an old man, many years later, but he had a very good memory. Thanks to Anna Coxe Toogood, Historian, Independence National Historical Park.

THE JOURNEY OF VENTURE SMITH

This journey is based on Venture Smith's memoir, *A Narrative of the Life and Adventures of Venture*, first printed in 1798. We do not know the exact location or look of Venture Smith's African home or of the slave castle he was taken to. Thanks to Dr. Charles L. Blockson, Afro-American Collection, Temple University; Dr. Catherine Clinton; John Singler, New York University.

DANIEL BOONE BUILDS THE WILDERNESS ROAD

This story is based largely on Felix Walker's narrative, written 49 years after the journey. Thanks to Jerry Raisor, Curator, Fort Boonesborough State Park; John Mack Faragher, biographer of Daniel Boone.

BRINGING THE BIG GUNS TO BOSTON

Henry Knox kept a day-by-day account of this journey in his diary. In 1976, 35 people reenacted the journey in 18 days, complete with cannons, mortars, sleds, and wagons. Thanks to Christopher D. Fox, Curator, Fort Ticonderoga Museum.

TO THE PACIFIC WITH LEWIS AND CLARK

The main sources for this journey are Clark's very detailed maps and the extraordinary journals of the expedition written by both Lewis and Clark. Thanks to Marlene Smith-Baranzini; Dr. James J. Rawls, Professor of History, Diablo Valley College.

DAME SHIRLEY GOES TO THE GOLD RUSH

Dame Shirley's letters were first published in a San Francisco magazine called *The Pioneer*. Thanks to Marlene Smith-Baranzini; Dr. James J. Rawls, Professor of History, Diablo Valley College.

WEST ON THE SANTA FE TRAIL

This journey is based on *Land of Enchantment: Memoirs of Marian Russell Along the Santa Fe Trail* by Marian Russell, © 1954, Branding Iron Press, 1981. Thanks to Robert Moore, New Mexico Press, reprinted by the University of New Mexico Press, 1981. Thanks to Robert Moore, Historian, Jefferson National Expansion Memorial; Andrea Sharon, Historian, Long Distance Trails Group, National Park Service.

BIG JOE BAILEY TAKES THE UNDERGROUND RAILROAD

Neither Joe Bailey nor Harriet Tubman was ever taught to write, but even if they had been, they would not have written about this journey at the time. To do so would have endangered the lives of everyone who helped them along the way. Many years later, when slavery was no more, Harriet Tubman told this story to Sara1 Bradford, who wrote it down for others to read. Thanks to Dr. Charles L. Blockson, Afro-American Collection, Temple University.

A CIVIL WAR JOURNEY

This journey is based on the unpublished letters of Orlando French to his wife, Lydia French. Thanks to Lora Emily Fuchs, great-great-niece of Orlando French, who has the letters today; Fred S. South, author of *It Never Recoiled: A History of the Seventy-Fifth Illinois Volunteer Infantry.*

JOHN MUIR WALKS AMERICA

John Muir wrote many wonderful books about his wanderings, including *A Thousand-Mile Walk to the Gulf.* Thanks to Dr. James J. Rawls, Professor of History, Diablo Valley College.

A COWBOY'S JOURNEY

This journey is based on the memoir of Baylis John Fletcher, *Up the Trail in '79,* edited by Wayne Gard (University of Oklahoma Press, 1968). Thanks to Robert Moore, Historian, Jefferson National Expansion Memorial.

ROSA CRISTOFORO COMES TO AMERICA

This journey is based on the story of Rosa Cristoforo Cavalleri, recorded by Marie Hall Ets in *Rosa: The Life of an Italian Immigrant,* © 1970 by the University of Minnesota, reprinted by the University of Wisconsin Press, 1999.

COAST TO COAST IN THE VIN FIZ

This journey is based on the story of Cal Rodgers as told in "Coast to Coast in 12 Crashes," by Sherwood Harris, *American Heritage,* October 1964.

LOUIS ARMSTRONG HEADS NORTH

Louis Armstrong loved to tell the story of his life. He wrote about this journey in his memoir, *Satchmo: My Life in New Orleans,* and told about it in an interview with Richard Meryman. Thanks to Dr. Carole Marks, Professor, Black American Studies, University of Delaware; Dan Morgenstern, Institute of Jazz Studies, Rutgers University; National Railroad Museum.

THE JOURNEY TO WORK

This journey is based on interviews with Graciela Moreno in New York. Thanks to Graciela Moreno for sharing her story with us; Kathy Schmelling, Reuther Library, Wayne State University; Roger Rosenthal, Migrant Worker Legal Action Program; Dr. Alice C. Larson.

LEAVING VIETNAM

This journey is based on interviews with Phong Bui in New York. Thanks to Phong Bui and his family for sharing their story and photographs with us.

Index